After Brexit?

Matthias Grebe | Jeremy Worthen (Eds.)

After Brexit?

European Unity and the Unity of European Churches

EVANGELISCHE VERLAGSANSTALT
Leipzig

Bibliographic information published by the Deutsche Nationalbibliothek
The Deutsche Nationalbibliothek lists this publication in the Deutsche Nationalbibliographie;
detailed bibliographic data are available on the Internet at http://dnb.dnb.de.

© 2019 by Evangelische Verlagsanstalt GmbH · Leipzig
Printed in Germany

This book is printed on ageing resistant paper.

Cover: Zacharias Bähring
Typesetting: 3w+p, Rimpar
Printing and Binding: Hubert & Co., Göttingen

ISBN 978-3-374-06157-0
www.eva-leipzig.de

Contents

Acknowledgements

We would like to express our thanks to the Evangelische Kirche in Deutschland (EKD), which with very generous financial support enabled the publication of this book as well as the event from which it emerged. Christoph Ernst and Manuela Barbknecht, our colleagues in the ecumenical office there, were ready to assist at every stage in bringing this project to fruition.

We are deeply grateful to the Archbishop of Canterbury, for hosting the "After Brexit" colloquium at Lambeth Palace and for being present throughout with his guest at that time, the President of the EKD Council, Bishop Heinrich Bedford-Strohm. Their contributions to the colloquium were of great value, while the Archbishop also made available after the colloquium an extended reflection on Europe and the churches for inclusion in this volume.

We are very appreciative of all those who participated in the colloquium and made it such a memorable and stimulating event. We are also conscious of our debt to colleagues from Church House and Lambeth Palace who worked with us on the design, planning and organization of the colloquium, especially Will Adam, Angeline Leung and Charles Reed.

Finally, we would not have been able to bring this book to publication in a timely manner without the dedication, attention to detail and administrative skill of Alice Costar, Research Intern at the Council for Christian Unity.

Matthias Grebe & Jeremy Worthen

1. Introduction

Matthias Grebe and Jeremy Worthen

The "After Brexit" Colloquium

The origins of this book lie in the concern to connect two distinct but related conversations: the conversation about European unity, which is primarily political,
social and cultural, and the conversation about the unity of the European churches,
which is primarily ecumenical and theological. In their current form, both conversations have their roots in the immediate post-war period; both offer reflections on achievements that seemed to have reached a certain level of maturity and
stability by the end of the twentieth century, and since that time both have become increasingly marked in variegated ways by tension and uncertainty. In the
case of the conversation about European unity, this tension and uncertainty were
dramatically heightened with the outcome of the United Kingdom's referendum
on leaving the European Union in 2016 and consequent preparations for "Brexit",
as it has come to be known. Those like the editors of this volume, who are directly
involved in the second conversation about the unity of the European churches, are
bound to wonder both what the implications of the changing nature of European
unity may be for the unity of the European churches, and likewise what the unity
of the European churches may have to say to those seeking a way forward for the
political, social and cultural unity of Europe at this critical juncture in its history.

It was with the aim of connecting those two conversations that ecumenical
staff at the Church of England and at the Evangelische Kirche in Deutschland
(EKD) conceived plans for a colloquium to bring together those individuals deeply
involved in each of them. The visit of the Chair of the EKD Council, Bishop Heinrich Bedford-Strohm, to the Archbishop of Canterbury, Archbishop Justin Welby,
in late 2018 provided an obvious context for holding such an event, and both
church leaders were present for the colloquium that took place at Lambeth Palace
on 16 November 2018. "After Brexit: European Unity and the Unity of the European Churches", supported by a generous grant from the EKD, brought together
politicians, church leaders and senior ecumenical figures along with researchers

and academics from a range of fields, including social and political sciences as well as theology. Over 60 people were present in total.

The day was structured to maximize time for discussion and interaction while also being informed by expert contributions from a number of the participants. These contributions were circulated in advance and then briefly introduced before responses and comments were invited. The first session, *The Church and the Unity of Society*, began with contributions from Ben Ryan and Arnulf von Scheliha, with Rosemary Nuamah Williams, the Archbishop of Canterbury's Social and Public Affairs Adviser, acting as the chairperson. The second session, *The Churches and the Unity of Europe*, brought together contributions from Gary Wilton and Piers Ludlow; the chairperson was James Walters, Chaplain and Senior Lecturer at the London School of Economics. The third session, on *The Unity of European Churches*, had a slightly different format. Two papers were circulated in advance, one from Sarah Rowland Jones, Dean of St Davids, and the other from staff at the Church of England's Council for Christian Unity, Will Adam, Matthias Grebe and Jeremy Worthen. After Rowland Jones had commented on her paper, there was a panel discussion facilitated by Guli Francis-Dehqani, the Bishop of Loughborough and Vice-President of the Conference of European Churches, between Nick Baines, the Bishop of Leeds, Robert Innes, the Bishop in Europe, Heikki Huttenen, the General Secretary of the Conference of European Churches and Sarah Rowland Jones.

Inevitably, passionate convictions were exchanged at various points over the course of the day about why Brexit was happening and what the United Kingdom should now do. It was invaluable in this context to have the benefit not only of a range of perspectives from across the United Kingdom but also to be in conscious dialogue with the EKD, and to hear views from those residing elsewhere within the European Union, including Belgium, France and the Republic of Ireland. The day ended with a session in which Bishop Bedford-Strohm and Archbishop Welby were interviewed together by Lord Wallace of Saltaire. What emerged from the event as a whole was a further doubling down of what is a significant attempt to establish key questions which the churches must face in the coming weeks, months and years. It drew out crucial themes for current discussions about what kind of European society the churches envisage for a post-Brexit future, and what the church's role should be in shaping it.

The main chapters of this book constitute papers that were prepared for the "After Brexit" colloquium and then revised in the light of the lively interchanges that took place. They are grouped under three headings: "History: the churches and the European Union"; "Context: European societies and the place of the church"; and "Response: what can the churches do?" This introduction uses these same headings to reflect on the discussion that unfolded during the day itself. It aims to identify critical issues, some of which receive substantial treatment in the chapters that follow, some of which are less prominent. All, however, are likely to require continuing attention in the coming years from those who share the view that the two conversations referred to above – about the political, social and cultural unity of Europe, and about the unity of the European churches – must find appropriate points of connection if the churches are to find their footing in a changing and often disorientating environment. Otherwise, they will struggle to understand properly their place in the current chapter of European history, and to witness effectively at this time to the joyful good news of peace and reconciliation in Jesus Christ.

History: the churches and the European Union

The sense of crisis about Brexit reached one of its peaks of intensity in the UK during the very week the colloquium was taking place. In such circumstances, it is easy for attention to narrow onto choices that must be made imminently and the issues that accompany them. Yet to understand where we are and the decisions that face us, we need to have some grasp of the history that has brought us to this point. Moreover, proposals for action in the present inevitably invoke a narrative about the past, and responsible decision-making requires us to be ready to reflect on its adequacy.

The roots of European integration

The colloquium presentations linked to the papers in the first part of this book both focused on the extent to which the churches played a role in the post-war origins of the project of European integration. Wilton focused on Robert Schuman's declaration of May 1950 as the original inspiration for the EU, with its primary aim of peace in Europe being sought by the practical mechanism of placing coal and steel production under a common authority, thereby making war materially impossible. While it was a political, not a theological, statement, Wilton maintained that the Schuman Declaration was nonetheless motivated by deep Christian faith and consequently could and should be read theologically. Its horizons extended beyond Europe: the solidarity sought within the European continent could also be extended across the Mediterranean Sea in concern for Africa. For Schuman, the creation of a supranational organization did not undermine nation states but enabled them to operate together to achieve common goals.

In his contribution to the same session, Ludlow agreed that religion was an important motivator for many of the key figures involved in the initial moves after World War II towards European integration. He also concurred that this did not reflect an ideological principle of weakening the nation state but rather two overriding concerns. The first was to avoid the relapse into deadly conflict that had swiftly engulfed the good intentions expressed by European leaders after World War I. The second was to address the new reality that political agency at the global level was shifting into the hands of non-European actors, in the form of the United States and the Soviet Union. In order to respond to these challenges, political leaders drew on pre-existing networks and connections, including, crucially, that of political Catholicism, or Christian Democracy, as it became in the post-war context.

Ludlow stressed, however, that there was little engagement with formal church bodies in this formative period, while explicitly religious language was studiously avoided in public statements. He argued that this reflected a recognition that in a context where political consensus was a priority, religion could be a catalyst for division, not least in that the Catholic Social Teaching on which Schuman and others naturally drew was an object of suspicion to many Protestants. The idea that Roman Catholics held an ambivalent approach to issues of national sovereignty was one that still resonated in some European societies, while it remained commonplace in the 1950s for Catholics to refuse so much as to pray the Lord's Prayer with other Christians. Of course, as well as divisions within Christianity itself, the further challenge remained of how to gain support from those who did not identify as Christians or who did not accept faith-based positions as a valid basis for modern political life. From the very outset, therefore, there was a reluctance to talk in explicitly religious terms about European integration, despite the critical role of religious motivations, reasoning and connections.

Inevitably, different rationales for participating in the project of European integration were influential for different European countries. In his presentation, von Scheliha emphasized the importance of the opportunity it represented for Germany's rehabilitation by the international community. Full participation in the emerging European institutions and eventually the EU was seen as a way to establish and stabilize democracy, advance the economy, reconstruct the country and seek peace and reconciliation with former enemies.

Ryan's paper highlighted the extent to which unresolved tensions around the role of religion in the origins of European integration continue to have an effect in the contemporary context. Affirming with Wilton and Ludlow the dependence of the great designers of the European project, such as Konrad Adenauer, Alcide De Gasperi and Jean Monnet as well as Robert Schuman, on Catholic Social Teaching, he proposed that:

> The European project was, in its origins, a Catholic ideological project. It is accordingly little surprise that it prompts a greater degree of scepticism from those whose politics and identity are inspired by a more Protestant intellectual tradition. The Church

of England and its adherents have tended to be closer to continental Protestants (particularly Scandinavians) than to Catholics when it comes to support for European integration.

It may not be accidental that the Church of England's historic (if now somewhat embattled) self-understanding as "the church of the nation" finds a strong parallel in the Scandinavian Lutheran churches. Ecclesial and national identities have been strongly intertwined in the past, even if they have been unravelling from one another for some time.

In some contrast to this historical picture, the colloquium demonstrated how far close involvement in European ecumenism today tends to be accompanied by strong support for European integration expressed in overtly religious terms. Yet the European ecumenists of the 1950s and 1960s were principally focused on how the unity of European churches across the "Iron Curtain" could make a significant contribution to European social and cultural unity that might offer a counterweight to the East-West division of the deepening Cold War. In this context, the closer integration of Western European nation states, aimed in part at increasing their political "reach" on the global stage in terms of economics and diplomacy, was more likely to attract suspicion than enthusiasm in those Eastern bloc countries to whose beleaguered churches Western ecumenists were seeking to reach out as a matter of urgency.[1] Rowland Jones, formerly a British Diplomat during the Cold war era and its immediate aftermath, suggested in a comment at the colloquium that this dynamic of suspicion on the part of Russia regarding European integration had been stirred up by both the fact and the manner of the expansion eastwards of the European Union and also NATO during the 1990s and 2000s. Historic tension between the project of post-war peace-building through European integration among member states of the EU and the concern for peace and solidarity across the European Continent as a whole now plays into a wholly different context. What are the implications for the European Churches in framing their current witness to peace and reconciliation, and in their striving for visible unity across Europe?

Eclipse of the post-war narrative

From the outset, the idea of European integration was presented as a means of binding together Western European nation states, whose conflicts had precipitated two world wars, into peaceful politics. Tensions would be resolved by other means than violence. The framing of European integration, including the creation

---

[1]   Lucian N. Leustean, *The Ecumenical Movement and the Making of the European Community* (Oxford: Oxford University Press, 2014).

of transnational institutions, as a project for peace was a crucial strategy in building support for it. While, as was stressed above, it was not cast in overtly religious terms, Christians could be expected to respond positively to this rhetoric. How can those who preach a gospel of peace be against the things that make for peace? And if the EU has – as its advocates routinely claim – assisted in sustaining an unprecedented era in the modern age of peace between the major European powers, how could the churches possibly fail to support it?

A number of participants in the colloquium expressed views along these lines. There were also some critical voices, however. Nick Baines, the Bishop of Leeds, spoke about growing up in the city of Liverpool when it was still marked by bomb sites: "you could look at the end of a terraced house and see the fire place on the second floor, because it had been bombed and there was a crater." For those who carry such memories, the imperative of embedding peaceful relations within Europe has immense force. As Baines pointed out, however, his children – and their children – do not share them: the repair to the city's landscape was complete by the time they were old enough to walk its streets. Of course, the presence or absence of memories of the effects of war does not determine the validity of arguments about whether the European Union has or has not made a contribution to fostering peace, but it does have a critical bearing on what he called "emotional, imaginative engagement". Baines' point was that the post-war narrative linking European integration and European peace has lost its power to inspire. If a new generation is to be motivated to sustain and deepen relations between different European societies, it needs to create a new narrative about what Europe could become – and why it matters. The failure so far to do that became evident, Baines suggested, in the debate within UK on its membership of the EU.

Jonathan Chaplin, a political theologian, also questioned relying solely on the post-war narrative about the EU ensuring peace in Europe, and thereby concluding that Christian faith compels support for it today. As he wrote in comments sent to the editors following the colloquium:

> There's a need to identify more precisely what it is we think political institutions, at any level, are for, what their "calling", capacities, limits and pathologies, are, and then whether there is some compelling political norm that justifies a transnational entity like the EU at all, how it needs to be reformed in the future in order better to fulfil its unique "calling", and then whether the UK itself should be part of it, and, either way, how it should construe its relation to the EU anyway.

Chaplin was not arguing that this is an impossible task, or that the answers would necessarily point away from the UK's membership of the EU (indeed, he himself is a convinced Remainer). His concern was rather that addressing these issues was a proper part of the churches' responsibility, and one which so far they had failed to take up. If for Baines the problem with relying on the post-war peace narrative for

European integration is that it has ceased to have compelling force as a narrative, for Chaplin the issue is that such rhetorical appeals cannot substitute for rigorous theological thinking about the purpose and value of political institutions.

In one of his responses to questions at the colloquium, Ludlow pointed out that the language of "the early idealism about Europe" associated with the beginnings of the post-war European institutions "was entirely directed towards internal European reconciliation". The difficulty in sustaining the power of that idealism, he suggested, is not only about fading memories of European war; it also concerns the changing character of the European population. For instance, many who live in Europe today do not identify the conflicts between European nations in the 20th century as their immediate history, or the legacy of those conflicts as their historic responsibility, for the simple reason that their arrival – or that of their family – in Europe occurred after they were finished. Europe has never been ethnically homogenous, but a narrative of reconciliation in which those represented as the principal actors do not reflect the ethnic diversity of the societies in which we live today is bound to seem increasingly remote.

A parallel point was made by Heikki Huttunen, General Secretary of the Conference of European Churches and also a priest in the Orthodox Church of Finland. He stressed that there is a plurality of narratives about Europe, with the narrative of Western European nations overcoming conflict and embarking on the successful path of economic and social integration – "now challenged by the fact of the Brexit" – only one of these.

> But there are other narratives of Europe too. The Eastern European communist parenthesis and everything after that, that's another other way of looking at Europe; the Southern European, the post-Ottoman and the Mediterranean story. And what about those stories that are usually not even written down, the Roma, they're a pan-European nation, but we hear very little about them or we don't have the ways to think in their terms.

Nonetheless, the UK has its own reasons for remembering that the absence of violent conflict is not something that can ever be taken for granted. Katy Hayward reminded other participants of the continuing fragility of the Northern Ireland peace process, and of the potential for it to be affected by changes to cross-border relations consequent on the UK leaving the EU and the associated political turbulence. In responding to her remarks, Ludlow noted that the EU had played a low-profile but nonetheless significant role at a crucial stage in the Irish peace process. It was an important reminder that whatever the value today of the post-war narrative about its origins in terms of the quest for lasting peace in Europe, the EU continues to have the capacity to support initiatives aiming to lessen tensions within and between its member states.

Context: European societies and the place of the church

Connecting the conversation about European political and social unity with the conversation about the unity of the European churches requires a careful analysis of unity within European societies today. Where are the tensions and the causes of fracture? What is it that underpins people's identification with their community or society, and how are boundaries of belonging being drawn between "us" and "them"? What is the role of religion and of religious actors, such as churches, in these processes, and what capacity exists for them to exercise significant influence? The second main part of the volume contains three chapters directly addressing these issues, which also attracted much interest at the colloquium itself.

Social divisions

Asked in the original briefing to reflect on "The Church and the Unity of Society" in (respectively) the UK and the German context, it was no surprise that social divisions should form a major theme in the papers for the colloquium from Ryan and von Scheliha. For Ryan, Brexit represented the crystallization of a number of long-term tensions that had come to characterize British society: between the generations, between town and city, as well as between different religious and ethnic groups. He proposed that the public space in which debates about Europe took place before, during and after the referendum had become "toxic" as social divisions hardened.

Ryan also noted the influential analysis of David Goodhart (present for part of the colloquium) that introduced a new division as key to understanding the emerging tensions in UK society: the division between "somewheres" and "anywheres", between those for whom place, community and identity are interwoven and those for whom they are readily separable.[2] Ryan then introduced his own variation on Goodhart's thesis. He suggested that a further line of division to have become visible in the referendum campaign was between those who talked in terms of "mind" and those who spoke in terms of "soul": those for whom rational arguments based on the knowledge of experts seemed self-evidently the most reliable basis for making such a significant decision, and those who were looking for a narrative about what had happened to their country and what might happen to it next in which they could readily locate themselves, on the basis of their experiences and perceptions.

---

[2]   David Goodhart, *The Road to Somewhere: The New Tribes Shaping British Politics* (Harmondsworth: Penguin, 2017).

Von Scheliha's balancing analysis of divisions within German society highlighted the contribution of two "crises": the financial crisis of 2008, and the so-called migration crisis that achieved particular prominence in Europe in 2015, when close to a million refugees entered Germany. Both fed into a deepening sense of alienation among those who were already feeling they had lost out socially and economically as a result of German unification. Associated with this was a growing gap between those living in rural and urban areas, as well as heightened attention to religious identity, with fears about Islam becoming prominent. These issues, covered for a long time by the relatively positive economic situation, were not adequately addressed in Germany's political sphere because Angela Merkel's long period of chancellorship in grand coalitions has absorbed an influential and strong parliamentary opposition and has had the creativity to identify problems. According to von Scheliha the refugee crisis works as a catalytic converter to bring the social problems into the open in recent years, as evident in the rise of the populist right, represented by the electoral success of a new political party, Alternative für Deutschland (AfD).

Other participants also emphasized the role of economic factors in social division. Robert Innes, the Church of England's Bishop in Europe, commented that "the UK's distribution of wealth, at least from a Continental perspective, highlights a staggering and totally unacceptable level of inequality, particularly compared to other Northern European countries." Guido de Graaff, a moral theologian working in the area of social and political thought, raised the broader question of how far people's lives are now being profoundly shaped by "very important global macro-economic forces" that are simply beyond the control not only of nation states like the UK and Germany but also of transnational institutions such as the EU. People may look to the EU as either saviour or villain in the current context, but how much influence can it exert in an age of economic globalization? Moreover, what power does the church really have to address these complex causes of social division?

In responding, Ludlow sounded a note of cautious optimism. He agreed that the great challenge facing contemporary European societies was no longer the prospect of intrastate war but rather that of economic globalization and its accompanying changes, which reach into people's everyday lives in all manner of ways. He affirmed, however, that European integration remains vital as one dimension of how European societies can respond to that challenge. Acknowledging that European leaders had not been very successful in communicating this, he suggested that the churches could have a role here. If economic changes lie at the roots of growing tensions and divisions within and between European societies, can European churches respond with effective testimony to human solidarity that reaches across national boundaries, and how it should inform economic policy and activity?

Place, identity and belonging

At various points in the colloquium, participants sought to articulate why it was that a majority of those casting a vote in the referendum had done so in favour of leaving the EU in 2016 – including, according to polling data discussed by Ryan in his chapter in this book, a majority of Christians. Indeed, self-identifying Christians appeared more likely to have voted to leave than the population average by a significant margin. Given the association of the EU via the post-war narrative with values such as peace, solidarity, reconciliation and cooperation for the common good, what led this to come about?

Different answers were given to this question, with a number of them exploring the relationship between place, identity and belonging. Ryan commented on polling data that located a key indicator of how people voted in the UK referendum in their response to two statements: (1) I no longer recognize the country in which I grew up, and (2) this country is a worse place now than it used to be. Those who disagreed with those statements were very likely to vote to remain in the EU. Those who agreed with them were very likely to vote to leave. In other words, people were wanting to leave the EU because of a positive attachment to their nation on the one hand and a negative assessment on the other of the trajectory on which it is currently travelling, with EU membership regarded as integral to that.

The significance of positive attachment to the nation as the primary motivation for many who voted to leave the EU was underlined by Philp North, the Bishop of Burnley. North commented that "it's easy to portray the Brexit vote as a negative anarchist thing, whereas in the North West it's a very positive vote for a vision of nation, in a place that's proud of flag, proud of nation, proud of armed forces, proud of the monarch, and so on. The European project is seen as, somehow, watering down, diluting, undermining, perhaps, that patriotic narrative." His assessment was paralleled by Rowland Jones' account of an older relative who was adamant about the need to leave the EU. Her reasoning had focused on a narrative of resilient national identity bound up with Britain's independence as an island not conquered by foreign invasion since 1066, but whose capacity to continue effectively delivering British well-being was diluted and threatened by its ties to the EU. In a very different context, Giles Fraser noted how the predominantly black congregation of his church in south London expect to pray for the Queen in the intercessions every Sunday. They too were proud of their country without embarrassment or ironic qualification.

Rowland Jones suggested there was an implicit theology here of the nation as the locus for experiences of both providence and redemption. Building on her comments, Fraser, who has made the case forcefully for Christians to support Brexit, drew a parallel with the State of Israel. For many Jewish people, its establishment in 1948 was a necessary response to the horrors of the Second World

War: rather than abandoning the nation state because of the perverted nationalism of Nazi Germany, Jewish people strove to build a nation state that could provide security against such evil in the future. Moreover, Fraser sought to ground the connection between place and belonging in the Hebrew Scriptures, which "have a very strong sense that love is particular." Indeed, he proceeded to say that it was also important to attend to that connection at a much more local level within the nation state, which nonetheless retained a crucial role in holding together the multitude of different communities in which place, identity and belonging were knitted together.

As North's observations quoted above indicate, it is not difficult for the national and the transnational to be seen as competing spheres for attachment and identity, as well as for sovereignty and power. More for one is taken to imply inevitably less for the other, so that those with a strong attachment to the national are bound to resist transnational attachments so far as possible. Two participants in particular, however, offered reflections that sought to explain how a strong sense of national identity need not be in tension with a strong sense of responsibility and belonging across national borders.

The first of these was the Bishop in Europe, who spoke of the inseparability of perceptions of self from perceptions of the other, citing Kipling's complaint: "What do they know of England, who only England know?" By stepping outside our own culture and seeing our country in the ways that others see it, Innes said, we gain a fuller and truer perspective on it, denied to those who remain wholly immersed in their society of origin. He then stressed the significance of multiple identities, arguing that in "a world of diversity and complexity", we have no choice but to hold different identities together in a way that allows them to be complementary to one another rather than in hostile tension. British people living in other European countries share the experience of many migrants around the world in holding dual "national" identities. Moreover, Innes proposed a role for the church here, in that Christians have always lived with multiple identities – as citizens of heaven, yet also members of earthly societies, as members of particular churches, and also members of the universal church.

Indeed, one might make a specific connection here to the ecumenical experience as "living in more than one place at once".[3] As Huttunen expressed it at the colloquium, the "attempt to hear more than one story is, of course, at the core of the ecumenical movement." There is perhaps a specific challenge here for hurches, such as the Church of England and the EKD (though rather differently), which have historically fostered a strong sense of overlap between ecclesial identity on the one hand and an identity of culture, society and place on the other. As North phrased it, can such churches find a way of "framing a narrative of nation

---

[3]   Keith Clements, *Ecumenical Dynamic: Living in More than One Place at Once* (Geneva: WCC, 2013).

that is tolerant, open and emphasizes unity?" Part of the answer to that question may be in terms of how they understand their own "borders" with other churches, and how they demonstrate freedom to cross them without loss of identity and belonging in their own "place".

The other contribution that resisted the idea of a necessary tension between the national and the transnational or international came from Bishop Heinrich Bedford-Strohm. He began by making a distinction between patriotism and nationalism: patriotism as pride in one's country, he claimed, is compatible with openness to remembering the dark aspects of its past in a way that nationalism that idealizes the nation is not. He described the roots of such patriotism as going very deep in human experience and as being an ordinary part of human flourishing: "of course, you should love your country. You should love your city. To have a home, it's wonderful. We call it 'Heimat' [...] a deep love and appreciation for what God has given to you. It's wonderful to feel at home." Yet when people move from loving their country in this way to believing it is superior to other countries, entitled to more than other countries and free to disregard the welfare of other countries, then something wrong and dangerous has occurred.

In order to articulate further how the "love of the particular" emphasized by Fraser need not be in competition with a love for all humanity across social boundaries, Bedford-Strohm explained his concept of "concrete universalism".[4] It is right that a father, for instance, would give more time and attention to the welfare of his own child than that of somebody to whom he is unrelated and whom he has never met. Yet it is that same love for his own child that generates sympathy for the situation of parents facing famine in other parts of the world who are unable to feed their children. "Love of the particular" enables recognition of the other as another like me in their particularity and their particular loves, and therefore as another human person who needs and deserves my help in the plight that confronts them. Bedford-Strohm concluded: "So there is no competition between universalism and concrete love of the people of your kinship. And to understand that and to, also, radiate it, in the way we speak about our global responsibility, I think, that is the task of the church."

Religion, society and plurality

The ambivalent role of religion in the post-war project of European integration has already been discussed. One of the questions that arises in the current social context is the extent to which secularization, ecumenism and the growth of religious plurality since then have fundamentally changed the situation regarding the

---

4   Cf. Heinrich Bedford-Strohm, *Liberation Theology for a Democratic Society: Essays in Public Theology*, ed. Eva Harasta (Münster: LIT Verlag, 2018).

potential contribution of the churches to the shaping of Europe. The combination of these developments means that the danger of tensions within and between European states being exacerbated by factors relating to their different Christian confessional traditions is very much reduced, if it has not quite disappeared altogether. Does that create new opportunities for the churches to speak and act in a European context today, despite diminishing resources and renewed controversy about the role of religion in public life?

What form those opportunities might take is the focus of the next section of the Introduction, but several participants commented on the relevance of the developments just referred to and how they are already altering the space for religious speech and action across European societies. On secularization, for instance, the Bishop in Europe reminded participants of the distinction drawn by Rowan Williams between procedural and programmatic secularism. Procedural secularism means that the state avoids giving preference to any one religious body, instead seeking to create a public square in which the variety of religious and non-religious actors can fully participate. In programmatic secularism, loyalty to the non-religious state is expected to supersede religious allegiance in the public square, where expressions of religious commitment and identity are unwelcome if not actually prohibited. For Williams, programmatic secularism presents a serious problem for Christianity, not least because it demands the restriction of religion to the "private" sphere, whereas procedural secularism does not.

The United States of America might be viewed as one example of procedural secularism in action, and indeed as proof that it needs not be inimical to religious flourishing. Malcolm Brown, Director of the Mission and Public Affairs for the Church of England, highlighted the historic tension for Britain of being pulled in two opposing directions: towards Continental Europe on the one hand, and across the Atlantic to North America on the other. In Europe, the nexus between religion, society and plurality became focused in the early modern era on preventing religious plurality from becoming a factor promoting violence within and between societies. The Elizabethan Settlement in England would be one example of this, with a certain degree of compromise taken for granted for the sake of social and ecclesial unity. The American situation, Brown argued, has generated a very different model, in which religious plurality is given a positive value: "when you look at American models of religion, especially within the Christian churches, a much more market-orientated approach seems to apply, of division and competition as a way of trying to establish religious truths." This is a model where, within a self-consciously plural society, religious plurality is nothing to be afraid of, and indeed a sign of religious health.

How much religious plurality, however, can be expressed within a plural society in the European context? A number of participants were mindful of voices asserting that the presence of Islam in particular cannot be readily accommodated alongside the diversity of Christian churches, and they were also concerned to challenge that perception. It was perhaps Toby Howarth, the Bishop of Bradford, who put the question here most sharply: "To what extent should the church welcome the religion of Islam at its place in the core of thinking about a European identity?" In offering a response, Huttunen wanted to resist the idea that dialogue with Islam inevitably weakens Christian identity. In fact, if Christians are to be welcoming to Muslims as those who also practice religion in plural Western societies, it is essential that they are not "ashamed or shy about being Christians." He also stressed, however, that "we have to discover the common history that we have on the European Continent. Islam is no newcomer to Europe, although, in our own townships and situations it may feel so." Moreover, however unfortunate the circumstances may sometimes be in which it has returned to prominence, "the question of religion and public space is a very timely one in many European situations, in many countries, in different ways. The society, the churches, the political people are looking for new ways to relate to the Christian heritage." The challenge in this situation is "how to make such a contribution which will help not only the Christian faith to remain in the picture as part of the cultural and social identity of the people, but how also to give space to all people of faith."

Response: what can the European churches do?

In the introduction he gave to his paper at the colloquium, Ryan offered a useful overview of possible ways in which churches can respond to situations in society that also applies to the challenges associated with Brexit. First, churches can engage with the communities around them, at local level and beyond. Second, they can support advocacy for those who are suffering because of what is happening in society, including those who find themselves marginalized. Third, they can help to develop and communicate a vision for society that is rooted in Christian teaching about justice, solidarity and the common good.

What resources do churches bring to this threefold task? In comments made after the colloquium, Chaplin stressed that they have the most to offer when they speak from their experience of striving for the kingdom of God in specific social locations. Their committed engagement in building community across a range of contexts, including those where it is profoundly challenging, shapes important insights into what is happening in society and how the gospel can be good news for it. The churches will rightly want to share those insights with others, including those who have responsibilities for government at various levels. While Chaplin recognised the need for churches to be involved in what Ryan referred to as advocacy and vision, he cautioned against them relying as they move into such territory on perceptions of the wider social situation that are not informed by rigorous theological thinking.

Community engagement

The role of the churches in building community is perhaps most readily associated with the local level of the village, town and city, and it may therefore seem rather removed from the challenges of European unity and the unity of the European churches that were the catalyst for the colloquium. At various points, however, participants underlined the importance of the church's calling to support varying forms of community life and relationship as critical in its response to the issues represented by Brexit.

Nicholas Hudson, Auxiliary Bishop in the Archdiocese of Westminster, reminded participants "that there are movements which have profoundly Christian origins and are engaging Christians and men and women of all sorts of different faiths and no faith in our midst in Europe, and which, in fact, we need to remember to nurture, announce and call to expand within this Continent." The particular example that he cited was that of the community of L'Arche, with its "most simple and yet profound vision of placing the most vulnerable members of society at the heart of our communities." The colloquium took place less than a week after the centenary of the World War I Armistice, and Hudson pointed out that "L'Arche was founded at Compiègne, just nestling close alongside the railway carriage in which the Armistice was signed." For Hudson, "L'Arche is prophetic," and calls the churches "to live the kind of prophetic witness that L'Arche is leading us in." Not everyone can live in committed communities of this kind, but they show us something of what the church can be seeking to foster in every place where it has been planted, and the kind of community it should itself aim to be.

One of the fruits of ecumenical encounter and dialogue is that different ecclesial and social communities come to know one another and be enriched by one another. Where that encounter takes place across national boundaries, then there is a further, potentially transformative dimension. This can take a variety of shapes: formal ecumenical dialogues and working groups; major events that bring Christians together from across the European Continent, such as the assemblies of the Conference of European Churches and the Community of Protestant Churches in Europe, or the German Kirchentag; links between dioceses, cathedrals, schools and seminaries; pilgrimage of various kinds, whether to historic destinations or to new spiritual centres such as the community of Taizé. Through such encounters, new communities are formed which, though they may be liminal and not enduring, can nonetheless transform the way that those who have entered them locate belonging to their "home" community within wider circles of belonging. Moreover, through the conversations they open up, churches become aware of common interests and concerns that may be addressed through more focused partnership working. One part of the churches' response to Brexit could be to identify and promote opportunities for such encounter and dialogue across both national and ecclesial borders.

This point was strongly affirmed by Graham Tomlin, Bishop of Kensington, in his reflections on the colloquium. He noted the development of "good links between the diocese of London, St Mellitus [College] and the Swiss Reformed Church over theological training and church renewal in recent years," suggesting that "this kind of friendship might be brought onto a more official footing and extended in other areas." In terms of how the colloquium might be followed up within the Church of England, he recommended that the church "explore ways in which partnerships can help foster European links across the churches, which will become even more important when political links become looser. Our common baptism is after all a stronger tie than a common logo on the front of our passports!"

The importance of the relationships that already exist and the need to sustain and develop them was also highlighted in the "Joint Statement" issued after the colloquium by Bishop Heinrich Bedford-Strohm and Archbishop Justin Welby:

> Since the Meissen Agreement of 1991 the Church of England and the *Evangelische Kirche in Deutschland* have, together, sought to find ways of strengthening ties between churches in England and Germany. Through parish and diocesan links, theological and educational exchanges we are able to see one another as brothers and sisters in Christ, united in our common baptism. If political and economic relationships are strained, it is the duty of Christians to work for unity and understanding and to build bridges between nations and cultures for the good of humanity, in the service of Jesus Christ.[5]

Advocacy

Many of those who spoke at the colloquium wanted to emphasize the churches' role in supporting those adversely affected by Brexit and the wider tendencies across Europe associated with it. There was widely-shared concern that we are likely to see new borders, new social divisions and a changing economic situation in the coming years. In this context, the churches have a duty to mitigate social divisions across Europe through fostering hospitality and social responsibility that extend beyond the boundaries of nationality. They should speak with a

---

[5]   Heinrich Bedford-Strohm and Justin Welby, "Joint Statement by the Archbishop of Canterbury and Landesbischof Dr Heinrich Bedford-Strohm," November 15, 2018, https://www.archbishopofcanterbury.org/news/latest-news/joint-statement-archbishop-canterbury-and-landesbischof-dr-heinrich-bedford-strohm.

unified prophetic voice that calls for placing the most vulnerable members of society at the heart of our communities.

There was, however, less consensus about where such advocacy should be focused, perhaps reflecting Chaplin's point that as churches move from community engagement to advocacy, they risk relying on social analysis that is inherently debatable. For von Scheliha, for instance, the first task of the churches in combating the social divisions in Europe that are likely to grow beyond Brexit was summed up as "speaking up for the long European period of peace building and reconciliation and the protection of human rights." Yet as was apparent in the discussion of "the post-war narrative" above, by no means all participants in the colloquium saw this as the best way to frame the churches' public contributions.

In his remarks at the colloquium, David Goodhart, whose influential analysis of British society has already been mentioned, challenged the church to focus on specific areas where its work of advocacy could have a significant impact on society. He spoke about the lack of recognition for full-time carers, despite the profound value of the work they do. His main emphasis, however, was on the family. Goodhart cited some sobering statistics on the high rates of family breakdown and also argued that the UK was out of step with most of Continental Europe (though not with North America) in its lack of fiscal support for the family. He wanted to see the church giving a much greater focus to supporting family life. This would be an example of how the churches' experience of seeking to maintain and strengthen community life could inform an advocacy role that includes being ready to make recommendations about social policy.

Goodhart was thinking primarily of the British situation, but his concern with how the churches' advocacy for specific groups within society might feed into the active shaping of social policy prompts the question of what this might mean at the European level. This was not directly addressed within the colloquium itself, although Ludlow suggested that once the UK falls outside EU institutions, different kinds of partnership – including that between churches – could acquire a new significance in enabling the UK's voice and influence to continue within European discussions. If Chaplin is right to argue that the church's advocacy is most effective when grounded in its community engagement, then it may be that it is from the kind of cross-European ecumenical relationships described above that priorities for the churches' European advocacy need to be discerned. That would also require, however, that ecumenical relationships enable a considered dialogue about the participating churches' community engagements, so that this shared experience and learning can inform their public advocacy in a transparent way.

Again, this area of response is picked up in the "Joint Statement":

This coming Sunday is *Volkstrauertag* in Germany – the annual commemoration of those who have died in armed conflicts. Our two nations have a history of war between us but also a history of the search for lasting peace. As some politicians and political forces seek to drive a wedge between people so it is all the more important that the churches continue to strive for reconciliation and to speak out prophetically for a Europe where the values of human rights and human dignity are central, based in the great Christian traditions of our two countries when at their best.

Vision

Linked to the discussion around the eclipse of the post-war narrative of European integration, a recurring theme at the colloquium was the lack of hope for the future in Europe at the present time, and how the churches might help to shape a hopeful vision of what Europe can now become. As von Scheliha emphasized, however, it is important to be clear about which Europe we are referring to in this context. Is the urgent task for the churches post-Brexit to foster a fresh vision for the EU, or for the countries of the European Continent as a whole? He urged participants to "be creative in finding a European perspective beyond the bureaucracy and lack of transparency in politics from Brussels. I think it's possible to find new visions, and it's necessary as well."

Chaplin was keen to press the question of how the churches understand the EU theologically as fundamental to any vision they might wish to promote about its future. He asked:

What are the prospects for the development of a Europe-wide political theology of the European Union as a political institution? I want to specify that I'm asking not for theologies of European culture, theologies of European cooperation, theologies of European solidarity; we have those, I think, in some abundance. It's a very specific question of a theologically grounded argument for the distinctiveness of the EU, which is a supranational entity.

He saw in the failure of the EU itself to articulate a justification for its shift from intergovernmental entity towards supranational authority one of the causes of the resistance to the EU that had found expression in the UK's vote for Brexit. Could the churches make a significant contribution to addressing that failure through some substantial theological thinking, or might they ultimately conclude if they examined the matter carefully that in fact there were good grounds for objecting to that shift?

The Catholic Social Teaching that inspired the founding figures of the EU would be an obvious resource for the project Chaplin was proposing. Other participants made use of key concepts from it, such as Jonathan Gibbs, the Bishop of Huddersfield, who proposed that a recovery of the idea of subsidiarity was needed for the renewal of the EU. The concept of solidarity, already mentioned several times, was also emphasized: can the churches develop an economic vision for post-Brexit Europe (and not just the EU) that is based on and promotes social relationships of solidarity?

At various points it was claimed that for any social vision offered by the churches to have credibility, it needed to be one that was actually expressed in the life of the churches themselves. This insight brings us back to the question that provided the catalyst for the colloquium and the book that has grown from it: what is the relation between the unity of Europe and the unity of the European churches? One answer would be to say: the lived unity of the European churches can show European societies what the social and political unity of Europe could mean. For this to be credible, however, the obstacles to unity between the churches would need to be addressed. Moreover, the churches are facing their own challenges to unity, as the papers in Part III of this volume explain. There is a loss of confidence in the goal of "full visible unity" as achievable or even, for some, desirable – certainly for those who think, with Brown's "American" model of religion and society, that religious competition is needed for religious health. In the churches as in society, there are groupings whose strong identity seems inseparable from opposition to other groupings, rendering conflict endemic. Ecumenists have preached the provisionality of denominational and confessional identities for a hundred years, but those identities have proved remarkably durable and show no sign of dwindling away just yet – indeed, it is arguable that the achievements of ecumenism have themselves provided triggers for their hardening.[6] Fear of loss of identity is clearly a factor in resistance to initiatives towards greater unity between churches, as it is with resistance to greater social and political integration within Europe, while in both ecclesial and political contexts there are those who would say that we already have enough unity, if not more than is really good for us.

In a context of widespread scepticism about the vision of the ecumenical movement, how can the European churches draw on their experiences of deepening relationships across confessional and national boundaries to speak to the societies where they belong? Mary Tanner, a veteran Anglican ecumenist, asked the Meissen Commission that supports the relationship between the Church of England and the EKD to reflect on:

---

[6]   Konrad Raiser, "The Nature and Purpose of Ecumenical Dialogue: Proposal for Study," *Ecumenical Review* 52:3 (2000): 287–92.

[...] what has been learnt about living together with unity and diversity in the last 25 years. What has that experience taught us about the making visible of the communion of God's life in our life as a sign for the world of its own possibilities? I don't think we can give up on visible unity though we need to refresh the portrait by emphasising more the diversity that blossoms in unity than we have done in the past and much more about the qualitativeness of life in unity, mutual accountability and the way of discernment together when hard issues threaten to tear us apart.

The desire for vision that can give hope for the future was also picked up in the "Joint Statement":

As religious leaders, united in our commitment to see a flourishing Europe committed to the common good and respecting the dignity of every human being, of all faiths and none, made in the image of God and the object of God's love in Jesus Christ, we call on our Governments not to lose sight of the urgent task of safeguarding our created world and its people. Our world requires a better future than one based in hatred and division. It is the task of the church to bear witness to the love of God, across borders as sisters and brothers in Christ.

Conclusion: Brexit and beyond

Since the 2016 referendum, it has become clear that Brexit is not only an event but a process: one with its dramas and crises, and its periods of relative calm and stability. Indeed, "process" may suggest a sense of focus and direction that could be misleading. While the UK is either in or not in the EU, and while there may be a date in history when it moves from one condition to the other, what it actually means for the UK to be outside the EU will continue to be the subject of political debate as well as institutional negotiation for years to come. It could take another decade before we are truly "beyond" Brexit, in the sense that the subject of its departure from the EU has become confined to the margins of political discussion in both the UK and the EU.

For the churches, one conclusion that might be drawn from the colloquium is that they need to move "beyond" Brexit in a different sense. Many church leaders – like many church members – have strong views on whether or not the UK should leave the EU, and on why Brexit is happening. There has never, however, been much scope for the churches to influence this political decision directly, at least since the referendum took place, and there is no immediate prospect of that situation changing. The challenge for the churches, therefore, is to move beyond the debate on the rights and wrongs of Brexit and discern what their response should be to it, and to the social situation that has both shaped it and continues to be shaped by it.

The contributions assembled in this book are intended to help the churches do that. They represent resources for the task, rather than its completion. Following this introduction, these chapters map out relevant history, context and potential responses, with a range and depth that are not matched in any other single volume at the time of publication. It is up to the book's readers, however, to judge how the European churches might act, in and from their unity, for the unity and well-being of Europe.

Bibliography

Bedford-Strohm, Heinrich, and Justin Welby. "Joint Statement by the Archbishop of Canterbury and Landesbischof Dr Heinrich Bedford-Strohm." November 15, 2018. https://www.archbishopofcanterbury.org/news/latest-news/joint-statement-archbishop-canterbury-and-landesbischof-dr-heinrich-bedford-strohm.

Bedford-Strohm, Heinrich. *Liberation Theology for a Democratic Society: Essays in Public Theology*, ed. Eva Harasta. Münster: LIT Verlag, 2018.

Clements, Keith. *Ecumenical Dynamic: Living in More than One Place at Once*. Geneva: WCC, 2013.

Goodhart, David. *The Road to Somewhere: The New Tribes Shaping British Politics*. Harmondsworth: Penguin, 2017.

Leustean, Lucian N. *The Ecumenical Movement and the Making of the European Community*. Oxford: Oxford University Press, 2014.

Raiser, Konrad. "The Nature and Purpose of Ecumenical Dialogue: Proposal for Study." *Ecumenical Review* 52:3 (2000): 287–292.

I History: The Churches and the European Union

2. Silent but Important: Religion as a Factor in the Integration Process

Piers Ludlow

For many Europeans, World War II and its immediate aftermath threatened to destroy all that they believed in. That this was the case for the years of war itself is perhaps not surprising. The Second World War, after all, involved not just the death of thousands of their fellow citizens and the physical destruction of so much of the continent's cultural and artistic heritage, but also for many a profound sense of guilt and responsibility for this new spasm of barbarism and bloodshed. Few influential Europeans could feel entirely untroubled by their own role in the continent's second descent into brutal and destructive war in half a century. This was made even more true once the full horrors of the Holocaust became clear. But this sense that all that they believed in was in mortal peril did not end on VE Day in 1945. On the contrary the manner of Europe's "liberation" and the fact that militarily it was mainly the work of two powers – the United States and the Soviet Union – that had traditionally been outside of, or peripheral to, European affairs, meant that the sense that European civilization was teetering on the brink of extinction endured deep into the later 1940s and early 1950s. The aims, objectives, and values espoused by either of the two emerging superpowers seemed profoundly out of step with, or alien to, the world view of most Europeans.

It was in response to this era of crisis, that many of Europe's leaders turned to ideas of European cooperation or unity. Such ideas long predated World War II of course.[1] Indeed there had been much discussion of how to promote European unity throughout the whole interwar period.[2] But the seriousness of Europe's predicament during the whole of the 1940s and into the early 1950s gave an unprecedented level of urgency to the notion of salvaging Europe's civilization and preventing a recurrence of internecine war through far-reaching cooperation

---

[1]   Anthony Pagden, *The Idea of Europe: From Antiquity to the European Union* (Cambridge: Cambridge University Press, 2002).

[2]   Peter M. R. Stirk, *European Unity in Context: The Interwar Period* (London; New York: Pinter Publishers, 1989). See also *Contemporary European History*, 26:2 (2017) & 27:2 (2018).

amongst European states and peoples. The fact that so many also saw nationalism in its most acute form as having lain at the heart of the disastrous wrong decisions taken in the 1930s that had plunged Europe and then the rest of the world into war, also gave the idea of "transcending the nation" through the quest for European unity an additional appeal.[3] It was therefore unsurprising that political and intellectual leaders across the continent sought to mobilize pre-existing intra-European networks in order to explore and promote European unity.

Amongst the most extensive and sophisticated of networks was that of political Catholicism or, as it would become more frequently known during the post-1945 era, Christian Democracy. Almost as soon as the war had ended, prominent figures within the emerging Christian Democrat parties that would play so central a role in the postwar politics of France, Italy, Germany, and the Benelux countries, had begun to meet regularly, often to discuss Europeanist ideas in the so-called Geneva Circle or the *Nouvelles Equipes Internationales* (NEI).[4] Crucially such fora helped re-integrate West German politicians back into some form of intra-European dialogue, long before the Federal Republic had come into existence or the postwar shape of Germany had become clear. And crucially too they allowed intra-European discussions to occur that were separate from the Four-Power talks about a European peace settlement, and then the Western Three Power deliberations about rebuilding Europe, where Anglo-American interests and preoccupations tended to prevail. This can only have encouraged a consciousness amongst Christian Democrat politicians of how many of the concerns and preoccupations they felt while seeking to rebuild their own countries were similar to, and linked with, the concerns of their neighbours, and an awareness of how different their fears and ambitions were from those of the Soviets, the Americans or even the British.

This immediate postwar pattern of intra-Catholic dialogue helps explain why the three national leaders most centrally associated with the birth of six-power integration from 1950 onwards were all Christian Democrats, and all figures extensively involved in the meetings of the Geneva Circle and NEI. Robert Schuman, the French Foreign Minister who gave his name to the first successful scheme for postwar European integration, Alcide De Gasperi, the Italian Prime Minister, and Konrad Adenauer, the first postwar German Chancellor, were all

---

[3]   This is one of the oldest debates in the integration history literature. See Wolfram Kaiser and Antonio Varsori, eds., *European Union History: Themes and Debates* (Basingstoke: Palgrave Macmillan, 2010).

[4]   Michael Gehler and Wolfram Kaiser, "Transnationalism and Early European Integration: The Nouvelles Equipes Internationales and the Geneva Circle 1947–1957," *The Historical Journal* 44:03 (2001): 773–98, https://doi.org/10.1017/S0018246X0100200X; Wolfram Kaiser, *Christian Democracy and the Origins of European Union* (Cambridge: Cambridge University Press, 2007).

deeply steeped in the traditions and thought patterns of postwar transnational dialogue amongst Catholics.[5] Indeed both Schuman and Adenauer had been involved in interwar discussions amongst Catholics, where again the idea of European cooperation had been repeatedly evoked.[6] Their readiness to press ahead with a bold and innovative scheme like the Schuman Plan, despite the non-participation and only thinly veiled scepticism of the British, was built in part on such ties. And each was also highly conscious of the way in which European cooperation seemed necessary to rescue the civilization of their continent from inexorable decline, if not extinction, and to provide a new focus for the energies and idealism of Europe's peoples. This in part helps explain why the rhetoric of peace and civilization that surrounded the launch of the Schuman Plan seemed to so far exceed the realities of launching a scheme to pool two important, but limited, sectors of heavy industry.[7] The first steps towards European unity were largely economic in nature, but their import and underlying significance were seen by their creators as extending far beyond mere commercial considerations.

Much less work has been done, by contrast, looking at intra-Protestant discussions and early European unity. Indeed, on the basis of today's historiography, if there is a counterpart to the role of Christian Democrats in the creation of the early European structures, it is most obviously to be found in discussions about European unity amongst socialists – although the weight of the initially sceptical British and Scandinavians within European socialism undoubtedly complicated socialist engagement with ideas of unity.[8] The other side of the political spectrum rather than the opposite side of the confessional divide has thus been seen as the more fruitful field for research. But there are some fragmentary indications of a Protestant role too. I was for instance very struck when examining a recent doctorate that listed the names of those who had chaired panels at a major Oxford Ecumenical (but mainly Protestant) conference in 1937, how many of the surnames

5   Raymond Poidevin, *Robert Schuman: Homme d'état*, 1886–1963 (Paris: Imprimerie nationale, 1986); Piero Craveri, *De Gasperi* (Bologna: Il mulino, 2006); Hans-Peter Schwarz, *Adenauer: Der Aufstieg*, 1876–1952 (Stuttgart: Deutsche Verlags-Anstalt, 1986).

6   Rosario Forlenza, "The Politics of the Abendland: Christian Democracy and the Idea of Europe after the Second World War," *Contemporary European History* 26:2 (2017): 261–86, https://doi.org/10.1017/S0960777317000091.

7   The language of the preamble to the eventual Treaty of Paris captures this contrast well, speaking of world peace, of Europe's contribution to civilization, of ending centuries-old rivalries, and of a destiny henceforward shared, before ending with the somewhat anti-climatic "have decided to establish a European Coal and Steel Community".

8   Talbot C. Imlay, *The Practice of Socialist Internationalism: European Socialists and International Politics, 1914–1960* (Oxford: Oxford University Press, 2018), 309–58.

were familiar from my work on later European integration history.[9] In many instances, I suspect it was a case of fathers and sons (or possibly uncles and nephews), rather than full individual continuity, but the presence of a Boegner, a Kohnstamm, a von der Gablentz, and a Marquess of Lothian was certainly suggestive. The one absolutely indisputable figure of continuity, moreover, in the form of John Foster Dulles, present in Oxford as a representative of US evangelicals but later US Secretary of State and major promoter of postwar European unity, was a reminder of how important certain strands of US Protestantism would subsequently become in encouraging European cooperation.[10] A detailed study probing the importance of Protestant networks in the postwar story of European cooperation is hence overdue.[11]

Christian Democracy and Catholic influences furthermore went on being important beyond the formative era of European integration in the 1940s and early 1950s, and into the 1960s, 1970s and 1980s. The most obvious connection of course continued to be the role of Christian Democrat politicians: no history of European integration would be complete without references to figures such as Helmut Kohl, Leo Tindemans, Wilfried Martens, Emilio Colombo, Aldo Moro, Giulio Andreotti, or Ruud Lubbers.[12] The gradual emergence of what is now the European People's Party, moreover, was crucial in consolidating a strong, highly pro-European majority within the increasingly influential European Parliament.[13] But even figures outside of the Christian Democrat family could play upon the language and symbolism of religion. Charles de Gaulle for instance, chose to make the centre-piece of his 1962 ceremonials (designed to cement Franco-German reconciliation and to signal to the French and German public the need to put past enmity aside), a joint Mass that he and Konrad Adenauer attended at the Cathedral in Reims – one of those many great European monuments badly damaged by the wars of the first half of the twentieth century but restored to their former glory

---

[9]   Tina Reeh, "The Church of England and Britain's Cold War" (D.Phil, University of Oxford, 2015), 83–84.

[10]   For more about Dulles' role see Pascaline Winand, *Eisenhower, Kennedy, and the United States of Europe* (Basingstoke: Palgrave Macmillan, 1996).

[11]   The new study by Leustean is helpful, but doesn't really suffice: Lucian Leuștean, *The Ecumenical Movement and the Making of the European Community* (Oxford: Oxford University Press, 2014).

[12]   For some of these see Wolfram Kaiser, *Christian Democracy and the Origins of European Union* (Cambridge: Cambridge University Press, 2007). See also Hans-Peter Schwarz, *Helmut Kohl: Eine politische Biographie* (München: Deutsche Verlags-Anstalt, 2012).

[13]   Pascal Fontaine, Hans-Gert Pöttering, and Joseph Daul, *Voyage to the Heart of Europe: 1953–2009: A History of the Christian-Democratic Group and the Group of the European People's Party in the European Parliament* (Brussels: Racine, 2009).

by the 1960s.[14] The European Commission President between 1985 and 1995, Jacques Delors, although a socialist, was also conspicuous in the extent to which he was influenced by Catholic social teaching and in his fascination with meeting with and talking to religious leaders.[15] He even appointed a theologian to the so-called *Cellule de Prospective*, the in-house mini think-tank that he set up within the Commission to think about Europe's medium to long-term development. And at the level of ideas, the notion of "subsidiarity", central to many of the debates about European integration in the final decade of the twentieth century, was plucked straight from Catholic social teaching, while the iconography of the European flag, adopted in the mid-1980s, may be traceable back to the circle of yellow stars often portrayed as surrounding the Virgin Mary's head in Spanish religious art especially.[16] Even in the wider Europe of the post-1973 period, the role of Christian thought in general and Catholic ideas in particular continued to be of some importance.

Despite such connections, however, explicit references to any religious motivation behind European unity, or to the importance of the continent's Christian heritage in explaining the urge to integrate, are more notable by their absence than their presence. Few European politicians chose to dwell at length on the role of faith in their actions; the European institutions themselves were even more reticent on the subject. Even high-level dialogue with religious bodies proved problematic. Gaullist France blocked the establishment of diplomatic ties between the European institutions and the Holy See until 1970.[17] There is thus a resounding silence about religion, in both the discourse within the European structures themselves, and in the wider debate about them. Given the prominence of Christian Democrat politicians in particular in the making of Europe, this is an apparent anomaly that needs to be explained.

The simplest explanation for this seeming silence where references to religion might have been expected to have been heard, is that most of those seeking to initiate the process of European integration were highly aware that they would only succeed were it possible to build a broad, multinational and transnational coalition in its favour, and that in such circumstances the potentially divisive topic of religion was best downplayed, or avoided altogether. Religion after all

---

[14] Jean Lacouture, *De Gaulle* (Paris: Seuil, 1984).

[15] The frequency of his meetings with religious leaders was a very noticeable feature of the papers of his private office in Brussels that I was asked to review a couple of years ago. They were exceeded only in number by meetings with trade unionists.

[16] Paul Marquardt, "Subsidiarity and Sovereignty in the European Union", *Fordham International Law Journal*, 18:2 (1994), 618–620.

[17] Lucian N. Leustean, "Roman Catholicism, Diplomacy, and the European Communities, 1958–1964," *Journal of Cold War Studies* 15:1 (2013): 53–77, https://doi.org/10.1162/JCWS_a_00308.

could easily have proved an additional factor dividing the founding members of the European Community from one another. A story from the early 1950s captures this potential problem well. In this period the Dutch briefly experimented with having two ministers of foreign affairs, one in charge of European affairs, the other responsible for relations with the wider world. The Dutch Prime Minister of the day, Willem Drees, had two names in mind but hadn't yet decided which of the jobs to allocate to each of them. At a formal dinner held in The Hague in honour of the Italian Prime Minister, Alcide De Gasperi, who was visiting the Netherlands as part of the ongoing diplomacy surrounding the European Defence Community project, Drees found himself sitting next to De Gasperi's daughter is who is meant to have commented how wonderful it was that the Six were building a Catholic Europe. Drees, a staunch Protestant, was not amused, and decided on the basis of this conversation to ask Josef Luns, one of the two individuals he was thinking of and who was Catholic to take the extra-European job, while Wim Beyen, a Protestant, was given the European job. Ironically, however, Beyen, despite being chosen for these reasons, turned out to be an enthusiastic European and the man generally regarded as the originator of the idea of a European economic community. He thus turned out to be much more pro-European than the rather more reserved and cautious Luns would have been. Furthermore, he is said to have converted to Catholicism on his death bed.[18] In this case then, Protestant anxieties about Catholic dominance turned out not to be too much of an obstacle to European advance, and possibly even a factor helping the European cause. But the story does nonetheless highlight how alive confessional sensibilities were in early postwar Europe – and how easily too overt a religious aspect of the integration process could have repelled some potential member states.

Too obvious a religious element would also divide countries internally. Confessional relations in the Federal Republic of Germany remained acutely sensitive; the CDU during the early postwar era was carefully seeking to position itself as a Christian party whose membership and electoral appeal stretched well beyond the purely Catholic base of the interwar *Zentrum* party. In such circumstances it was certainly not wise to talk about "building a Catholic Europe". Nor would even a more broadly defined "Christian Europe" help garner the type of broad base of support that the early integration process needed. In the early postwar years, religious affairs were a notorious flashpoint in France, Belgium and the Netherlands, liable to provoke sharp divisions between those close to the church and those who saw themselves as fully secular. Both Belgium and the Netherlands were noted for their "pillar" system, with society deeply divided into Catholic, socialist and liberal "pillars". In France too the notion of *laïcité* was central to the political system. Furthermore, as noted above, there was also a strong socialist

---

18   Anjo G. Harryvan, *In Pursuit of Influence: The Netherland's European Policy during the Formative Years of the European Union, 1952-1973* (Brussels: Peter Lang, 2009).

constituency in favour of European unity, which would be wholly repelled were any hint given that the Europe that the politicians of the centre and centre-right wanted was a "Europe of the Vatican". The European cause could only fulfil the hope of many like Adenauer, and become a focal point for the energies and aspirations of most young Germans, French or Italians if it were defined in a non-partisan, non-confessional fashion. And this was all the more so, were there any hope, as many in Europe still liked to think, of broadening the integration process and winning back British support and participation.[19]

It was hence much safer to focus either on the technocratic aspects of building Europe or, if a more idealistic objective needed to be pointed to, concentrate on Europe as a peace project.[20] Transcending the nation state so as to avoid the recurrence of European war was a goal that appealed to many of those who were motivated in part by religious considerations. But it was also a broad aspiration that could be shared by Catholic and Protestant alike, by clerical and lay, by left and by right, and by theists and atheists. The Cold War context also meant that 'Europe' did not need to find an internal "other" against which it could define itself, but instead had a ready-made external threat. The fact that Communism was "godless" was certainly something that could be used to fire the enthusiasms and passions of some Christian Democrat audiences during the 1950s in particular.[21] But there were many other aspects of the Soviet Union that were equally frightening and threatening for those without religious belief, so it was politically more astute for Western European politicians and ideologues to seek a much broader response by defending "freedom" and "liberty" rather than "Christianity". Interestingly, Rosario Forlenza has recently shown how the concept of the *Abendland*, a German term much used in Catholic circles to describe those aspects of Catholic European culture under threat from modernity and liberalism more generally, came to be redefined in the 1950s and 1960s as an embattled Cold War West threatened from without by Communism rather than from the modernizers and reformers within.[22] But a similar redefinition of the threat occurred on a much broader level, encouraging the battle to save European

---

[19]   For the resilience of continental hopes that Britain would change its mind and join a process it had initially shunned, see N. Piers Ludlow, *Dealing with Britain: The Six and the First UK Application to the EEC*, Cambridge Studies in International Relations 56 (Cambridge: Cambridge University Press, 1997), 12–48.

[20]   For a recent discussion of this theme, see the forum on "European Integration as a Peace Project", *British Journal of Politics and International Relations*, 19:1 (2017) 3–12.

[21]   Paolo Acanfora, "Christian Democratic Internationalism: The Nouvelles Equipes Internationales and the Geneva Circles between European Unification and Religious Identity, 1947–1954," *Contemporary European History* 24:3 (2015): 375–91, https://doi.org/10.1017/S0960777315000211.

[22]   Forlenza, "The Politics of the Abendland."

civilization to be waged in a fashion that could attract support from across the Western European political spectrum and not just from those organized in religiously affiliated political parties. Highlighting the notion of a religious Europe, of whatever type, would hence be deeply counterproductive.

The two partial exceptions to this rule only serve to highlight the factors that helped dampen if not mute entirely references to religion elsewhere in European politics. The first was the way in which Italian Christian Democrat rhetoric went on throughout the 1950s at least, but also to some extent beyond, referring quite openly to the importance of a shared Catholic heritage as a building block for European integration.[23] This however reflected two realities of the Italian situation that did not prevail elsewhere. The first was that, despite a tiny Protestant minority, Italy was more religiously uniform than any other of the founding members of the European Communities. There was hence no likelihood of such references to Catholicism worsening intra-confessional relations. And second, Italy's socialists, uniquely amongst Western European countries, initially sided with the Communists on the question of Italy's international and Cold War alignment, pushing them, until the late 1950s at least, effectively beyond the political pale. As a result, the need to soft-pedal the religious aspect so as to maintain support from the socialist party and from socialist voters did not apply until after the EEC had been created in 1957. The Italian exception, therefore, does more to underline the general rule than to break it. Similarly, the only much more recent example of an EU member state (or more precisely in this case, a soon-to-be member state) that has campaigned vociferously and publicly for greater attention to be paid to Europe's Christian heritage was the Polish government during the European Convention of 2002–3 which drafted the EU's abortive constitution. At several points during these negotiations both the Vatican and the Polish government pressed hard for a reference to God to be included in the Convention, perhaps in the preamble, only to be staunchly resisted by the majority of their counterparts. Once more however it is surely significant that this campaign was conducted by a country that was preparing to join rather than one socialized in the long-established habits and patterns of behaviour of the Community/Union.[24] The insiders were well aware that this was an issue to skirt around cautiously; it was thus left to a total outsider (the Vatican) and a state on the threshold of membership to make most of the running on the question. That the alliance between the Pope and the Poles did not succeed, furthermore, also underlines the strength of the consensus to draw a veil of silence around the question of religion.

The silence surrounding Europe's Christian roots and the general disinclination to tackle religious issues head-on, was also made much easier by the nature of

---

[23] Acanfora, "Christian Democratic Internationalism."

[24] Peter Norman, *The Accidental Constitution: The Story of the European Convention* (Brussels: EuroComment, 2005).

the EC/EU's agenda during the twentieth century at least. The early Community and even the EU of comparatively recent times could afford not to deal with religion, in other words, because the issues on which it focused attention were not ones which necessitated much heed to be taken to the issue. Until the early 1970s, after all, the Community's core business centred overwhelmingly on trade and agriculture, neither of them issues where direct engagement with the churches was necessary or helpful. From the 1970s onwards this minimalist agenda began to grow steadily, encompassing new fields like monetary integration, environmental policies, redistribution from wealthier states to poorer areas, and even limited cooperation over foreign policy. But even here there was little scope or need for an overt religious dimension. This was especially true as the direct contact between the EC institutions and the wider public remained minimal. Farmers, fishermen and some industrialists needed to go to Brussels frequently; most citizens of the EC member states did not, including therefore church groups. The Community's first efforts to define its core values, furthermore, were wholly restricted to the secular fields (whatever their longer term origins) of human rights and a commitment to democracy.[25] It was hence only really in the 1990s, and still more in the early years of the twenty-first century, as the Union, now vastly expanded in policy scope as well as in membership, began tackling questions such as education or citizens' rights and attempted to broaden its interaction with civil society, that the question of how to engage with religious structures became impossible to duck altogether. Even here, though, the cautious language of Article 17 of the 2008 Treaty of Lisbon, speaks volumes about the strong level of circumspection that remains over this issue:

1. The Union respects and does not prejudice the status under national law of churches and religious associations or communities in the Member States.
2. The Union equally respects the status under national law of philosophical and non-confessional organizations.
3. Recognizing their identity and their specific contribution, the Union shall maintain an open, transparent and regular dialogue with these churches and organizations.

Likewise, the reference to religious heritage in the preamble of the same Treaty is careful in the extreme and highly unspecific: "Drawing inspiration from the cultural, *religious* and humanist inheritance of Europe, from which have developed

---

25   Emma De Angelis and Eirini Karamouzi, "Enlargement and the Historical Origins of the European Community's Democratic Identity, 1961–1978," *Contemporary European History* 25:3 (2016): 439–58.

the universal values of the inviolable and inalienable rights of the human person, freedom, democracy, equality and the rule of law."[26]

So where does this leave us in 2018? The basic answer is probably that the disinclination of the EU either to refer explicitly to its Christian heritage or to highlight the role of religion in its making remains every bit as strong now as it has ever been. Some of the intra-confessional sensitivities of the 1940s and 1950s have faded, it is true. But in their place has arisen a much greater sensitivity on the part of virtually all moderate European politicians and civil servants to the potential dangers of talking about religion in multi-cultural societies, populated by a huge variety of different faith-groups and by many of no religion at all. In a Europe that is already deeply divided and preoccupied with the issue of migration, and where many of the migrants and asylum seekers come from Muslim countries such as Syria, there is little incentive for mainstream politicians or for those representing the EU, to brave the dangerous terrain of talking extensively about Europe's Christian roots. This is made all the more so by the fact that virtually the only European politicians who do talk frequently about religion and who underline Europe's Christian heritage, are conservative and populist leaders in Poland, Hungary or Matteo Salvini's Italy, using such rhetoric to stoke Islamophobic sentiment. Even initiating a discussion of this subject would hence be seen as conceding ground to extremists who few in the political centre ground want to encourage. The topic is best left in the silence that has surrounded it since 1950.

The fact that the EU leaders and its institutions are likely to remain wary about talking overtly about religion or about Europe's Christian heritage does not however mean that there is no scope for fruitful cooperation and dialogue between the European structures and organized religion about what Europe should stand for and what its policies should be. On the contrary, I think there has been a growing awareness for some years now that the European Union needs to broaden its appeal and talk more convincingly about the non-economic rationale for European cooperation. In an age of rising identity politics and populism, appealing just to the economic self-interest of European citizens is unlikely to be sufficient. After all, as the Brexit referendum forcefully reminded us, the economic calculations of those who seek to outline the financial and commercial benefits of European integration may not be believed – or even if they are believed, voters may still choose to value non-economic factors like sovereignty or the desire for cultural uniformity more highly than the material rewards that integration might bring. The longest standing argument about the non-material benefits of integration, namely the peace argument referred to above, is also in danger of losing

---

[26]   Both quotations are drawn from Sergei A. Mudrov, "Religion in the Treaty of Lisbon: Aspects and Evaluation," *Journal of Contemporary Religion* 31:1 (2016): 1–16, https://doi.org/10.1080/13537903.2016.1109863.

some of its potency in a Europe where few have any direct memories of anything other than peace. For Europeans who have never experienced war, the notion that by pooling sovereignty their governments made war amongst them "materially impossible" may no longer seem of any great relevance.

Europe therefore needs to construct an appealing message about what it stands for, what values it seeks to protect, and what aspects of its civilization are distinctive and worth preserving. This message will no doubt have to be framed in a secular and non-religious terms, for all of the reasons outlined above. But this does not mean that it is a message that cannot be influenced either by groups connected to the churches and to organized religion, or by politicians some of whose motivations derive from their religious convictions. On the contrary, the fact that Europe needs to move the terrain upon which it justifies itself, from the predominantly economic to a broader set of values, provides a real opportunity for those groups whose own purpose is to reflect about values, about civilization and about the deeper meanings of life, to have a significant and important voice in the debate.

Bibliography

Acanfora, Paolo. "Christian Democratic Internationalism: The Nouvelles Equipes Internationales and the Geneva Circles between European Unification and Religious Identity, 1947–1954." *Contemporary European History*. 24:3 (2015) 375–91. https://doi.org/10.1017/S0960777315000211.

Birchfield, Vicky, John Krige, and Alasdair Young. "European integration as a peace project." *The British Journal of Politics and International Relations*. 19:1 (2017): 3–12.

Craveri, Piero. *De Gasperi*. Bologna: Il mulino, 2006.

De Angelis, Emma and Eirini Karamouzi. "Enlargement and the Historical Origins of the European Community's Democratic identity, 1961–1978." *Contemporary European History* 25:3 (2016): 439–58.

Fontaine, Pascal, Hans-Gert Pöttering, and Joseph Daul. *Voyage to the Heart of Europe: 1953–2009: A History of the Christian-Democratic Group and the Group of the European People's Party in the European Parliament*. Brussels: Racine, 2009.

Forlenza, Rosario. "The Politics of the Abendland: Christian Democracy and the Idea of Europe after the Second World War." *Contemporary European History* 26:2 (2017): 261–86.

Gehler, Michael and Wolfram Kaiser. "Transnationalism and Early European Integration: The Nouvelles Equipes Internationales and the Geneva Circle 1947–1957." *The Historical Journal* 44:3 (2001): 773–98. https://doi.org/10.1017/S0018246X0100200X.

Harryvan, Anjo G. *In Pursuit of Influence: The Netherland's European Policy during the Formative Years of the European Union, 1952–1973*. Brussels: Peter Lang, 2009.

Imlay, Talbot C. *The Practice of Socialist Internationalism: European Socialists and International Politics, 1914–1960*. Oxford: Oxford University Press, 2018.

Kaiser, Wolfram and Antonio Varsori, eds. *European Union History: Themes and Debates.* Basingstoke: Palgrave Macmillan, 2010.

Kaiser, Wolfram. *Christian Democracy and the Origins of European Union.* Cambridge: Cambridge University Press, 2007.

Lacouture, Jean. *De Gaulle.* Paris: Seuil, 1984.

Leustean, Lucian. "Roman Catholicism, Diplomacy, and the European Communities, 1958–1964." *Journal of Cold War Studies* 15:1 (2013): 53–77. https://doi.org/10.1162/JCWS_a_00308.

Leustean, Lucian. *The Ecumenical Movement and the Making of the European Community.* Oxford: Oxford University Press, 2014.

Ludlow, Piers. *Dealing with Britain: The Six and the First UK Application to the EEC.* Cambridge: Cambridge University Press, 1997.

Marquardt, Paul. "Subsidiarity and Sovereignty in the European Union." *Fordham International Law Journal.* 18:2 (1994): 618–620.

Mudrov, Sergei A. "Religion in the Treaty of Lisbon: Aspects and Evaluation." *Journal of Contemporary Religion.* 31:1 (2016): 1–16. https://doi.org/10.1080/13537903.2016.1109863.

Norman, Peter. *The Accidental Constitution: The Story of the European Convention.* Brussels, EuroComment, 2005.

Pagden, Anthony. *The Idea of Europe: From Antiquity to the European Union.* Cambridge: Cambridge University Press, 2002.

Poidevin, Raymond. *Robert Schuman: Homme d'état. 1886–1963.* Paris: Imprimerie nationale, 1986.

Schwarz, Hans-Peter. *Adenauer: Der Aufstieg, 1876–1952.* Stuttgart: Deutsche Verlags-Anstalt, 1986.

Schwarz, Hans-Peter. *Helmut Kohl: Eine politische Biographie.* München: Deutsche Verlags-Anstalt, 2012.

Stirk, Peter M. R. *European Unity in Context: The Interwar Period.* London; New York: Pinter Publishers, 1989.

Reeh, Tina. "The Church of England and Britain's Cold War." D.Phil, University of Oxford, 2015.

Winand, Pascaline. *Eisenhower, Kennedy, and the United States of Europe.* Basingstoke: Palgrave Macmillan, 1996.

3. A Re-Reading of the Schuman Declaration for a Post-Brexit Era

Gary Wilton

Introduction

If the UK leaves the European Union it will mark a unique reversal in the history of post-1945 Europe. For seventy-three years the history of the continent has been epitomized by a seemingly irreversible momentum for successive enlargements of the European Union, and idealized by a narrative of peace and reconciliation. Although the 2007 Lisbon Treaty made provision for member states to leave, no one actually expected that it would ever happen. Not least David Cameron the architect of the UK's 2016 referendum. Nonetheless a reversal has happened and an era, however brief, of separation and contraction is about to begin. This is now a key moment to re-examine much of what has been taken for granted for the past 65+ years including the very ideals of the EU's founding fathers.

The post-1945 generation of statesmen dreamt of founding a new Europe at peace with itself and freed from the ravages of war. Drawing on the work of Jean Monnet and working in collaboration with the West German Foreign Ministry, Robert Schuman, the French foreign Minister anticipated a pan-national community that would embed peace across the continent. Central to his proposal was the placing of the primary means of waging war – coal and steel – under a common High Authority, thereby making war "materially impossible."[1] It was the political expression of the Christian ideals of forgiveness and reconciliation and the precursor to permanent peace.

Although surprisingly brief, the Schuman Declaration, made at the Quay d'Orsay on 9 May 1950, thus had at its heart a radical proposal for economic solidarity as the means of achieving and sustaining peace. The succeeding 60 years have been marked not only by peace and reconciliation between historic adversaries, but also by unprecedented economic prosperity; and the creation of the world's only multi-national democracy involving 28 member states with a

---

[1]   See Transcript at the end of this chapter.

population of 500 million people.[2] Although Schuman's ostensible focus was on coal and steel, his underlying concern was to embed democracy in Europe as the guarantor of peace. For Schuman, democracy owed its existence to Christianity with its commitment to human dignity, freedom and love.[3]

Europe's Christian inheritance

The public expression of Christian faith was part and parcel of the era in which Schuman and the other co-founders of the EU lived and worked. Politicians would make unembarrassed reference to God or prayer or the Church. Even Winston Churchill, who described himself as more a buttress than a pillar of the Church of England made frequent public reference to the Christian faith.[4]

The Christian Church is the most extensive and longest enduring institution in Europe. For nearly two millennia the Roman-based Church legislated across the cultural and linguistic boundaries of the continent. Even after the Reformation, the Roman Catholic Church retained its international reach but now contested the public space with new civil authorities, and the new national Churches. In the eighteenth century the reaction against traditional forms of authority led to the emergence of the Enlightenment model of universal secular legality. In different parts of Europe, Catholic universalism and the common traditions of custom and mutuality were replaced with a system of legally framed equality and freedom largely separated from religious sanction. Nonetheless the Churches continued to jostle for space, quarrelling and making deals with the state authorities and each other. In the process they shaped the public space and the shared values of the continent.

The former Archbishop of Canterbury Rowan Williams argued that the complex and evolving relationships between the Churches, common law, canon law and Romanized law meant that political power in Western Europe was the subject of negotiation and balance. The power of the state could be questioned by the Church and was restrained by feudal and other obligations to the people. The Christian history of the continent is not solely about the history of the faith but also the history of a political argument. A political argument which was less about

---

[2]   See "Living in the EU," last modified December 20, 2018, http://europa.eu/about-eu/facts-figures/living/index_en.htm.

[3]   See Jeff Fountain, *Deeply Rooted: The Forgotten Legacy of Robert Schuman* (Heerde: The Schuman Centre for European Studies, 2010), 41.

[4]   See R. Crosby Kemper, *Winston Churchill: Resolution, Defiance, Magnanimity, Good Will* (Missouri: University of Missouri Press, 1996), 199.

debating the appropriateness of Church–State relationships – and more fundamentally about the sharing and shaping of public space.[5]

The State is restrained by law and from a Christian perspective is also answerable to God. The whole political sphere lies open before God. Those who act within it are ultimately accountable to a power higher than any human assembly. Notions of pluralism, creative engagement with the state and recognized limitations on the power of the state underpin democracy! Williams noted, "Europe is what it is because of its Christian history,"[6] even if at times the Church resisted liberalizing developments. "Reformation and Enlightenment protests upon which much of modernity in Europe rests did not come from nowhere; they were centrally theological disputes, even when they were resolved in ways inimical to the authority and public influence of faith. If we are unaware today of this background, we shall misunderstand where the liberal tradition comes from; and we shall be more than ever vulnerable to the sort of unhistorical optimism."[7]

The presence of the Church has been a persistent reminder that the state does not have ultimate claims on its subjects. The state should always be under scrutiny and history should always be seen as still unfolding, still unfinished.When religious communities are acknowledged as partners in public debate, their creative engagement with secular authorities is likely to lead to authentically European outcomes. Doing so knowingly is not a sign of theocratization, but rather the opposite – healthy and constructive pluralism. Dialogue with the Church, religious communities and other values-based organizations enables the Union to engage with its inherited values with integrity and to recognize their contributions to contemporary economic, financial and ecological thinking.

The contemporary significance of the Schuman Declaration

Robert Schuman made his Declaration at a time of considerable economic and political instability. The Europe of 1950 was still economically, socially and politically scarred by the Second World War and the breakdown of relationships with Soviet Russia raised the possibility of a third world war. The way forward had to be communal, international and possibly federal. Long-standing economic competitors and military foes would need to cede something of their national independence to build a common future.

In the Schuman Declaration we see an outline sketch of one such communal way forward – one shaped by the particular challenges of the post-World War II

---

5   Rowan Williams, *Faith in the Public Square* (London: Bloomsbury, 2012), 75–84.

6   Ibid., 78.

7   Ibid., 79.

period and also shaped by an indelible Christian understanding that all women and men are made and called to love and help one another, and to live in peace. For 65+ years the peace and reconciliation narrative has informed the EU's re-unification and enlargement agenda. The UK's vote for Brexit shattered this comfortable orthodoxy and now requires an urgent re-reading of the declaration in preparation for an era of separation and contraction – where relationships that have previously been shaped by the putting down of old barriers need to be re-calibrated and rearticulated in advance of the new barriers that are to come. In what follows I offer a theologically-orientated commentary on the Declaration to demonstrate how Schuman's embryonic vision still shapes much of the contemporary European Union and wider thinking, and may continue to shape public engagement and common purpose of the churches of Europe after Brexit. The full text of the Declaration follows this chapter.

World peace

> World Peace cannot be safeguarded without the making of creative efforts proportionate to the dangers which threaten it. The contribution which an organized and living Europe can bring to civilization is indispensable to the maintenance of peaceful relations [...].
>
> The solidarity in production thus established will make it plain that any war between France and Germany becomes not merely unthinkable but materially impossible [...].
>
> [...] this proposal will lead to the realization of the first concrete foundation of a European federation indispensable to the preservation of peace.[8]

The opening sentences of the Schuman Declaration make clear that peace was its primary aim. Peace in Europe needed to begin between France and Germany and would impact the rest of the world.

The desire for world peace is shared by the world faiths and by secular humanists. In the Christian tradition it is found at the heart of the beatitudes. Christians also understand that the Atonement of Christ offers to the world the hope of universal peace and reconciliation. This hope has been the inspiration for generations of Christian peacemakers.

The genius of Schuman's peace-making proposal was to move away from military solutions to the shared control of economic resources. The removal of the means of making war from France and Germany would make peace not only

---

[8]   See Transcript of The Schuman Declaration at the end of the chapter.

achievable but sustainable. Whilst NATO[9] inherited the military responsibility for western European security, the embryonic European Community focused first on coal and steel and subsequently on wider economic, social and political cooperation as the key means of sustaining peace.

The ultimate success of Schuman's approach was the eventual integration of countries from the former Soviet bloc into the EU.[10] Each stage of the enlargement of the European Community extended peace across the continent. Peace may have become the norm between EU member states, but terrorist activity in various capital and regional cities is a reminder that Europeans still need to work together in the face of new and different threats. Russia's 2008 invasion of Georgia and 2014 annexation of Crimea warn that the peace enjoyed by most of Europe is not yet the norm for everyone.

Other parts of the world continue to be riven by war. In 2007 the European Commission launched its Instrument for Stability to strengthen its work in the areas of conflict prevention, crisis management and peace building.[11] Projects include mediation, confidence building, interim administrations, developing the rule of law, transitional justice or the role of natural resources in conflict. Under its Peace-Building Partnerships the Commission seeks to strengthen civilian expertise for peace-building activities.

Such international activities are far beyond Schuman's prophetic imagination. The EU has gained global respect for its soft activities. In 2012 the EU was awarded the Nobel Peace Prize[12] for its contribution to peace. This was met with both joy and derision. Those who responded with joy readily acknowledged Schuman's legacy, while those who responded with derision, rightly pointed out the lack of peace in Cyprus and the EU's impotence in relation to Syria.

Within the union, the churches have energetically contributed to the soft activities that embed peace. The Commission of Bishops' Conferences of the

---

[9]   See the official website of the North Atlantic Treaty Organization, http://www.nato.int/history/index.html.

[10]   Such as Bulgaria, the Czech Republic, Hungary, Poland, Romania and Slovakia 2004 followed by the three Baltic states that had been part of the Soviet Union, Estonia, Latvia and Lithuania in 2007; "Further Expansion," accessed February 21, 2019, http://europa.eu/about-eu/eu-history/2000-2009/index_en.htm.

[11]   See "Regulation (EC) No 1717/2006 of the European Parliament and of the Council of 15 November 2006 Establishing an Instrument for Stability," *Official Journal of the European Union*, accessed February 14, 2019, https://ec.europa.eu/fpi/sites/fpi/files/documents/regulation_1717_2006_15_11_2006_en.pdf.

[12]   "European Union Receives Nobel Peace Prize 2012", accessed February 18, 2019, https://europa.eu/european-union/about-eu/history/2010-today/2012/eu-nobel_en.

European Community [COMECE][13] and the Conference of European Churches [CEC][14] have worked extensively across the continent to strengthen relationships between Churches and across political divides. The long established and extensive work at Coventry Cathedral[15] is a model of Church-based reconciliation ministry. While for a twenty-first-century Europe where the integration of Muslim communities is a major concern, the work of the St Ethelburga's Centre for Peace and Reconciliation in London[16] is also a model that policy-makers might do well to emulate.

Here it is important to be reminded that much of the post-war era peace in Europe was lived out under the cloud of possible conflict between the Soviet East and the liberal democratic West. While East and West sought to balance the threat that they posed to each other, the churches through CEC, COMECE and others created pan-European structures which crossed the divide in order to nurture ongoing relationships and to help sustain peace.

While Brexit does not threaten peace, it is a new divide, with all the potential to create a new *them* and *us* where misunderstanding and even hostility can grow. It will be important for the churches of the UK to resist withdrawing into an island bunker and to continue to work together with the churches of the Union and beyond in support of peace – both in Europe and in the wider world. Here the priority given to promoting international peace and reconciliation by the current Archbishop of Canterbury Justin Welby will be key.[17] At the same time the churches of the UK may need the pro-active friendship of the churches of the Union even more than at present to help sustain their European and Global perspectives.

Unity in Europe

In taking upon herself for more than 20 years the role of champion of a united Europe, France [...].

Europe will not be made all at once, or according to a single plan [...].

---

[13]   See the official website of The Catholic Church in the European Union, http://www.co mece.org/.

[14]   See the official website of The Conference of European Churches, http://www.ceceurope. org/.

[15]   See "Our Reconciliation Ministry", accessed February 18, 2019, http://www.coven trycathedral.org.uk/wpsite/our-reconciliation-ministry/?doing_wp_cron=1550216269. 118755102157592773437.

[16]   See "About Our Work," accessed February 18, 2019, https://stethelburgas.org/who-we-are/about-our-work/.

[17]   See "Reconciliation," accessed February 1, 2019, https://www.archbishopofcanterbury. org/priorities/reconciliation.

The coming together of the nations of Europe requires the elimination of the age-old opposition of France and Germany. Any action must in the first place concern these two countries [...].

[...] a first step in the federation of Europe.[18]

Closely linked to peace, Schuman stated that the nations and people of Europe should be *united*. Beyond his specific proposal for coal and steel, he did not delineate what a united Europe might look like, and used the word federal without giving it substance. The process of European (re)-unification would be evolutionary and voluntary. From the beginning, the project was facilitated by the deliberate vagueness. A vagueness that enabled member states to progress their own interests and to find common cause with others. Not surprisingly in every decade of its history the community has been beset by questions of identity, purpose and destination.

For much of the second half of the twentieth century Europe was even more divided than is popularly recognized. The division of the Soviet-controlled East from the West until 1989, is easily remembered. However, the totalitarian regimes of Southern Europe, Greece, Portugal and Spain were also a distinctive block, while another group had declared themselves avowedly neutral: Austria, Finland, Ireland, Sweden and Switzerland. Prior to 1973 the UK stood alone and looked to its transatlantic and commonwealth relationships. In 2013, the non-celebration of the 40th anniversary of the UK's accession to the common market was a clear sign that the UK's ill-ease with *Europe* was growing apace. The vote for Brexit has been accompanied by a call for a global Britain and a return to old transatlantic and commonwealth *certainties*.

Enlargement of the Union was paralleled by concern for *unity* with non-members of the community. This is particularly apparent in its European Neighbourhood Policy designed to strengthen relationships with neighbouring states post 2004 and embedded in the 2014 European Neighbourhood Instrument.[19] The Union offers a *privileged relationship* with neighbouring states on the basis of a mutual commitment to democracy and human rights, rule of law, good governance, market economy principles and sustainable development. The stronger the commitment to shared values the more the EU invests in its neighbourhood relationships.

---

[18] See Transcript of The Schuman Declaration at the end of the chapter.

[19] See "Regulation (EU) No 232/2014 of the European Parliament and of the Council of 11 March 2014 Establishing a European Neighbourhood Instrument," *Official Journal of the European Union,* accessed January 18, 2019, https://eur-lex.europa.eu/LexUriServ/ LexUriServ.do?uri=OJ:L:2014:077:0027:0043:EN:PDF.

After Brexit, the UK would be not only a non-member but a newly dis-united or divorced former member. Geographically, economically and politically the UK undoubtedly would be a very near neighbour. But a very different neighbour to those included in the 2004 Neighbourhood policy. In the midst of the divorce negotiations there has been a clear and repeated political rhetoric about the UK having a "deep and special relationship"[20] with the EU. Nonetheless divorce is never easy and the process of drawing up and finalizing of most divorce settlements can be so difficult and full of rancour that it is often impossible to resume amicable relationships. Here there is a risk that tensions may remain high until the current generation of politicians complete their terms of office.

It will be important that any such rancour does not spill over into the churches, particularly those with national affiliations.

The Schuman Declaration, as the founding document of the EU, addresses only nation states. By 1957 the shared experience of the European Coal and Steel Community led the Treaty of Rome to speak of "an ever closer union between the peoples of Europe."[21] The challenge for the member states and the institutions of the expanded Union of the twenty-first century is to give meaningful expression to the unity of the Union and to nurture the engagement of the citizens. To stay healthy, a united Europe needs to continue to seek "effective partnership with the component communities of the state, including religious bodies."[22] Such partnership, with its inevitable place for dialogue with the Churches, could make a significant contribution to the healing of the democratic deficit that besets the Union.

The disunity and the unity of the churches may parallel the disunity and unity of the European nation states. The Roman Catholic, Orthodox and Protestant traditions are institutionally dis-united and will be so indefinitely. Nonetheless they can model unity in their relationships, partnerships and shared advocacy both to the *remaining* members of the Union and to the *leaving* UK.

The sharing of sovereignty

Franco-German production of coal and steel as a whole be placed under a common High Authority, within the framework of an organization open to the participation of the other countries in Europe [...].

---

[20] Phillip Hammond and David Davis, "Joint Article: A Deep and Special Partnership," accessed January 18, 2019, https://www.gov.uk/government/news/joint-article-a-deep-and-special-partnership.

[21] "The Treaty of Rome," accessed February 1, 2019, https://ec.europa.eu/romania/sites/romania/files/tratatul_de_la_roma.pdf.

[22] Williams, *Faith in the Public Square*, 84.

By pooling basic production and by instituting a new High Authority, whose decisions will bind France, Germany and other member countries [...].

The common High Authority entrusted with the management of the scheme will be composed of independent persons appointed by the governments, giving equal representation. A chairman will be chosen by common agreement. The Authority's decisions will be enforceable in France, Germany and other member countries. Appropriate measures of appeal will be provided for against the decisions of the Authority.[23]

The issue of sovereignty was never far away from the UK's Brexit referendum. And never far from the EU founders' minds. The creation of the common High Authority over the coal and steel industries was key: "Never before have states entrusted, nor even envisaged delegating a fraction of their sovereignty to an independent supranational authority."[24] Somehow Schuman managed to combine national self-interest with a wider shared interest. Membership of the Community would be open and the Europe envisaged was to be shaped by self-determination. In contrast to the episodes of military occupation and the imposition of rule by one nation over another, the new Europe would be open and voluntary. Smaller nations, demonstrably more vulnerable to military threat, would have the same right to membership as their larger neighbours.

Schuman argued that the creation of a supranational organization did not undermine the nation state but enabled it to operate on a broader and higher plane. But free membership did not mean that members of the community could opt in and out. The nations of Europe would be bound together by international treaty and would need to negotiate for their own needs in relationship to their partners. Key to building confidence would be a binding appeals procedure. The ceding of power to an arbiter with binding authority was a requirement on all and vital to the creation of a Common High Authority. If the Common High Authority was the forerunner of the European Commission, the arbiter was the forerunner of the Court of Justice of the European Communities based in Luxembourg.

Although regularly confused with the European Court of Human Rights based in Strasbourg, the role of the Court of Justice is to uphold Community law. It arbitrates between EU member states, EU institutions, businesses and individuals. For Schuman, "the rule of law safeguarded a common heritage and argued that every person placed under its jurisdiction should enjoy human rights and fundamental freedoms." This "created the foundations of a spiritual and political

---

[23] See Transcript of The Schuman Declaration at the end of the chapter.

[24] Robert Schuman, "Opening Speech at the Schuman Plan Conference in Paris, 1950," accessed February 27, 2019, http://users.belgacombusiness.net/schuman/bio-details.htm.

cooperation, from which the European spirit will be born, the principle of a vast and enduring supranational union."[25]

The sharing of sovereignty between victor and vanquished countries in the creation of common institutions was a remarkable expression of forgiveness and reconciliation. Nonetheless the creation of the European Court of Justice was the political recognition that the nations of Europe are as vulnerable to *sin* as they ever were.

With a proud imperial past and as the major European victor of the Second World War the UK has struggled to share sovereignty through its membership of the EU and the Council of Europe. For many Leave voters Brexit was primarily energized by the desire to escape from the interference of Brussels and to rule ourselves, "to take back control."[26]

Concepts of human agency and the taking of responsibility for our own actions are deeply embedded in Christian theology. But so are concepts of cooperation, mutuality and the common good. Going forward the churches will need to applaud the taking of responsibility for self, but also to speak prophetically where care for self excludes the responsibility to care for others.

Solidarity within Europe

It will be built through concrete achievements which will first create a de facto solidarity [...].

The pooling of coal and steel production should immediately provide for the setting up of common foundations for economic development [...].

The setting up of this powerful productive unit, open to all countries willing to take part and bound ultimately to provide all the member countries with the basic elements of industrial production on the same terms, will lay a true foundation for their economic unification [...].

In this way, there will be realized simply and speedily that fusion of interest which is indispensable to the establishment of a common economic system [...].

The task with which this common High Authority will be charged will be that of securing in the shortest possible time the modernization of production and the improvement of its quality; the supply of coal and steel on identical terms to the

---

[25]   Robert Schuman, "The Definition of the New Europe – Speech Made at the Signing of the Statutes of the Council of Europe, St James Palace, London, 1949," accessed February 27, 2019, http://users.belgacombusiness.net/schuman/5May1949.htm and http://users.belgacombusiness.net/schuman/HumanRights.htm.

[26]   "It's the Slogan, Stupid: The Brexit Referendum," accessed February 1, 2019, https://www.birmingham.ac.uk/research/perspective/eu-ref-haughton.aspx.

French and German markets, as well as to the markets of other member countries; the development in common of exports to other countries; the equalization and improvement of the living conditions of workers in these industries.[27]

At the end of the Second World War, Europe was economically and politically broken. Even the politically strong UK was economically exhausted and near bankrupt. From this shared poverty the declaration sought to facilitate the sharing of the fruits of economic reconstruction. Although France and Germany were identified explicitly, all of Europe was invited to participate, with the more powerful nations encouraged to work mutually and creatively with the less powerful.

The shared horizontal and vertical reconstruction of coal and steel industries was designed to ensure equality of supply to France and Germany. Schuman argued that this would lead to a *de facto* solidarity and interdependence, by binding national interest with a shared interest. The successful integration of coal and steel would also create the foundations for further shared and peaceable economic development.

The two key tools for furthering solidarity have been the Common Agricultural Policy and Regional Policy. The Common Agricultural Policy [CAP] was established by the 1957 Treaty of Rome. It was designed to support a struggling agricultural sector and to secure food supplies. From the outset the CAP was a German recognition of its relative industrial strength and an expression of support for politically powerful but vulnerable French farmers. Regional policy gained fresh impetus after the 1992 Maastricht Treaty which led to a new Structural and Cohesion policy designed to aid the weaker economies within the Union. By 2013 regional policy accounted for 35 % of the total EU budget.[28] In 2010, the 12 members who joined the Union between 2004 and 2007 received more than half of Cohesion and Structural Funds (52 %).[29] The same countries received nearly 20 % of CAP funding.[30]

The 2008 economic and financial crisis impacted all the member states and those in the south and east in particular. The natural response for each of the member states is to focus on their own problems. The challenge for the EU as a whole is to ensure that expressions of solidarity between member states are translated into actions which make a real difference to the lives of the most vulnerable citizens of the whole continent. Inspired by Catholic Social Teaching, this is a very natural place for the churches to speak out together, including across the post-Brexit divide.

---

[27] See Transcript of The Schuman Declaration at the end of the chapter.

[28] See "Available Budget 2014–2020," accessed February 19, 2019, http://ec.europa.eu/regional_policy/thefunds/funding/index_en.cfm.

[29] Ibid.

[30] Ibid.

Solidarity with the wider world

> This production will be offered to the world as a whole without distinction or exception, with the aim of contributing to raising living standards and to promoting peaceful achievements. With increased resources Europe will be able to pursue the achievement of one of its essential tasks, namely the development of the African continent.[31]

Here Schuman's concern extended to Africa, aware as he was of French and other European colonial interests. This was the beginning of the current EU relationship with Africa with its various expressions of solidarity, including development aid, support for civil society and the promotion of human rights.

Often linked to European colonial activity, the Churches have extensive links with Africa and have a longstanding concern for the sustainable development of the continent. Two months prior to British accession to the Community, the Church of England's General Synod debated *Britain in Europe*. This report emphasized the need for the European Community to "make a more effective contribution to the improvement of living standards in the developing countries" and saw this as "one of the most important of the opportunities which membership of the Community will bring."[32]

In his 1983 *Windows onto God*, the then Archbishop of Canterbury, Robert Runcie, declared:

> If you picture the world as a great ocean liner, then most of Europe is sitting in the First class dining rooms. Unfortunately, water is pouring into the steerage where the poorer passengers are huddled. The captain and crew must take some time from devising ever more sophisticated menus for the first-class passengers in order to deal with this threat to the whole ship. My hope for the Churches of Europe is that they will not be found saying grace in the first class compartment as the ship sinks, but will be trying to raise the alarm. If we fail with the problems of the steerage we shall not remain insulated from the effects of the incoming water for ever.[33]

In 2005, the British Prime Minister, Tony Blair, challenged the European Parliament to make development a much higher priority.[34] The EU, together with its member states, is the world's largest donor of Overseas Development Aid (ODA). It accounts for more than half of the world's efforts. Giving three times as much to

---

[31]   See Transcript of The Schuman Declaration at the end of the chapter.

[32]   A Joint Report by MPA and CCU, "GS 1548: The Church of England and Europe Report," 2004, 41.

[33]   Robert Runcie, *Windows onto God* (London: SPCK, 1983), 159.

[34]   See "Blair's European Speech," June 23, 2005, accessed February 27, 2019, http://news. bbc.co.uk/2/hi/uk_news/politics/4122288.stm.

developing countries – as a proportion of GDP – as the US. Yet the EU continues to struggle to join up its aid, climate change, trade, judicial, diplomatic, military and other policies. With regard to Africa, in 2000 the Africa–EU Partnership was established to enable the EU and the countries of the African continent to work together in support of the millennium development goals. Since 2007 the Partnership has adopted three successive roadmaps and action plans. Following the fifth AU-EU Summit of 2017 in Abidjan, cooperation is currently focused on *Investing in Youth for a Sustainable Future.*[35]

The 2008 economic and financial crisis had a disproportionate impact on Africa. Although the continent only has limited linkages with the world's financial systems, reduced demand for African products led to lower earnings. African economies suffered a $578 billion reduction in export earning between 2009 and 2011; representing 18.4 % of GDP[36] and five times the aid expected by the continent during these two years. Earnings from tourism and capital flows were also much reduced. Such a massive external shock has impacted hard-won progress towards the Sustainable Development Goals.

At the same time, climate change presents an ever-increasing threat to the people of Africa and demands increasing solidarity of the EU and the UK. In his address to the General Synod of the Church of England in July 2015, the current Archbishop of Canterbury stated:

> We need to be deeply engaged in the development, as we are through the Anglican Alliance, of the new SDGs, the Sustainable Development Goals. If climate change is to have the place that it needs in international policy, conflict is one of those areas that destroys any attempt to manage issues around climate change. Climate change is both a driver of conflict and a victim of conflict, and we must face that reality and use our networks to address that issue.[37]

The churches with their global reach and the particular access that they have in sub-Saharan Africa have significant expertise and resources to offer in partnership with the EU and the national government development agencies. To date the UK has been particularly proactive in the areas of climate change and sustainable

---

[35] See "Final Declaration AU-EU Summit," accessed February 1, 2019, https://www.con silium.europa.eu/media/31991/33454-pr-final_declaration_au_eu_summit.pdf.

[36] Jean-Claude Maswana, "The Global Financial Crisis and Recession: Impact on and Development Prospects for Africa," Working Paper No. 15, 2010, Japan International Cooperation Agency Research Institute, https://www.jica.go.jp/jica-ri/publication/working paper/jrft3q00000022yl-att/JICA-RI_WP_No.15_2010.pdf.

[37] "Church Must 'Look Outwards' to Tackle Climate Change, says Archbishop," accessed October 9, 2018, https://www.archbishopofcanterbury.org/speaking-and-writing/speeches/church-must-look-outwards-tackle-climate-change-says-archbishop.

development as well as a committed provider of International Aid, working both independently and alongside EU partners. Here the churches will want to continue to work together to encourage both the EU and the nation states to build on their existing global commitments.

Working with the United Nations

> A Representative of the United Nations will be accredited to the Authority, and will be instructed to make a public report to the United Nations twice yearly, giving an account of the working of the new organization, particularly as concerns the safeguarding of its objectives.[38]

Perhaps this element of Schuman's Declaration, more than any other, is a child of its time. It expressed an over-confidence in the embryonic United Nations. Schuman could not have imagined that the proposal for a European Coal and Steel Community might develop into a political union of 500 million. Brussels has become a global capital with the highest concentration of diplomats in the world – higher than in New York, the seat of the United Nations. Rather than needing to account to the United Nations the EU normally acts in UN negotiations as a single body. The EU has a permanent delegation in New York while the UN also has a substantial presence in Brussels. The UN and EU present themselves as the closest of partners:

> The European way is also the United Nations' way. This explains why all our actions, all our initiatives are always taken in full coordination and partnership with the UN. We believe in the UN, because we believe in the same principles, in the same values, and our communities are built upon the same fundamental ideals.[39]

The EU is an unnumbered extra player at G7, G8 or G20 gatherings. The President of the Commission and the President of the Council sit alongside Heads of State or government at such events. As well as being an economy of global significance, the EU brings its commitment to human rights and sustainable development, and belief in a law/rule-based approach.

---

[38]   See Transcript of The Schuman Declaration at the end of the chapter.

[39]   "The European Union at the United Nations, Fact Sheet," last modified September 21, 2018,   https://eeas.europa.eu/headquarters/headquarters-homepage/9875/european-union-united-nations_en.

Europe cannot without contradicting itself, indulge in crude power projection else-where in the world at the expense of the virtues of self-limitation, compromise and submission to the laws that underpin European integration. Rather it must seek to export these virtues. It is no coincidence that Europe's foreign policies have met with their rare successes mostly when European positions expressed values of engage-ment, respect for the rule of law and multi-lateralism.[40]

In a world where religion is an implicit as well as explicit element of international relationships, and sometimes key to understanding interactions between differ-ent actors, it is important that the EU's European External Action Service and indeed the churches engage with the complex relationships between religion, development and foreign policy.

Whilst being aware that religion, including the Christian Church, is part of a world broken by violence and disorder, the Church proclaims a gospel of peace. This is the peace between God and humanity, brought about by Christ who is him-self our peace,[41] which brings hope to people in the direst of situations. It impels the followers of Jesus to act as peacemakers,[42] by prayer for the world, by working for reconciliation and by seeking to establish justice whose fruit is peace. Here the Churches need to be mindful of their responsibilities in the area of reconciliation and of the resources and insights to which they have to contribute.

How the European churches maintain their relationships and their working for the common good post-Brexit, whether it be at the United Nations or the Coun-cil of Europe or elsewhere, needs to be and can only be Good News for the world.

Conclusion

The Europe that gave birth to Schuman, De Gasperi, Monnet and Adenauer had been profoundly shaped by the Christian Church. Inspired by their faith the founding fathers of the Europe Union shared the Christian ideals that all women and men are made in the image of God; that all people have an inviolable sacred worth and dignity. Following from this, men and women are made and called to love one another and to live in peace.

The presence and persistence of the Christian Church within 2000 years of European history not only embedded Christian values within the cultural life of the continent but also contributed to the shaping of the public realm. The exis-tence of the Church has been a constant reminder that the state does not have

---

[40] Giles, Andreani, "Europe's Uncertain Identity," accessed February 21, 2019. https://www.cer.eu/publications/archive/essay/1999/europes-uncertain-identity.

[41] See Eph 2:14.

[42] See Matt 5:9.

ultimate claims on its subjects. Democracy, freedom and the rule of law are accepted values in Europe, because of the Church. "Europe is what it is because of its Christian history."[43]

For more than 65 years the Christian-inspired peace and reconciliation narrative has informed the EU's re-unification or enlargement agenda. In 2016 the UK's majority vote for Brexit shattered this comfortable orthodoxy and requires a re-reading of the declaration for a chapter of separation and contraction. Churches serving continuing and even the departing member(s) of the European Union would benefit from renewed inspiration from the EU's founding vision, purpose and values. Re-examination of the Schuman Declaration is a good place to start.

The Schuman Declaration

World peace cannot be safeguarded without the making of creative efforts proportionate to the dangers which threaten it.

The contribution which an organized and living Europe can bring to civilization is indispensable to the maintenance of peaceful relations. In taking upon herself for more than 20 years the role of champion of a united Europe, France has always had as her essential aim the service of peace. A united Europe was not achieved and we had war.

Europe will not be made all at once, or according to a single plan. It will be built through concrete achievements which first create a de facto solidarity. The coming together of the nations of Europe requires the elimination of the age-old opposition of France and Germany. Any action taken must in the first place concern these two countries.

With this aim in view, the French Government proposes that action be taken immediately on one limited but decisive point.

It proposes that Franco-German production of coal and steel as a whole be placed under a common High Authority, within the framework of an organization open to the participation of the other countries of Europe. The pooling of coal and steel production should immediately provide for the setting up of common foundations for economic development as a first step in the federation of Europe, and will change the destinies of those regions which have long been devoted to the manufacture of munitions of war, of which they have been the most constant victims.

The solidarity in production thus established will make it plain that any war between France and Germany becomes not merely unthinkable, but materially impossible. The setting up of this powerful productive unit, open to all countries willing to take part and bound ultimately to provide all the member countries with the

---

43   Williams, *Faith in the Public Square*, 78.

basic elements of industrial production on the same terms, will lay a true foundation for their economic unification.

This production will be offered to the world as a whole without distinction or exception, with the aim of contributing to raising living standards and to promoting peaceful achievements. With increased resources Europe will be able to pursue the achievement of one of its essential tasks, namely, the development of the African continent. In this way, there will be realized simply and speedily that fusion of interest which is indispensable to the establishment of a common economic system; it may be the leaven from which may grow a wider and deeper community between countries long opposed to one another by sanguinary divisions.

By pooling basic production and by instituting a new High Authority, whose decisions will bind France, Germany and other member countries, this proposal will lead to the realization of the first concrete foundation of a European federation indispensable to the preservation of peace.

To promote the realization of the objectives defined, the French Government is ready to open negotiations on the following bases.

The task with which this common High Authority will be charged will be that of securing in the shortest possible time the modernization of production and the improvement of its quality; the supply of coal and steel on identical terms to the French and German markets, as well as to the markets of other member countries; the development in common of exports to other countries; the equalization and improvement of the living conditions of workers in these industries.

To achieve these objectives, starting from the very different conditions in which the production of member countries is at present situated, it is proposed that certain transitional measures should be instituted, such as the application of a production and investment plan, the establishment of compensating machinery for equating prices, and the creation of a restructuring fund to facilitate the rationalization of production. The movement of coal and steel between member countries will immediately be freed from all customs duty, and will not be affected by differential transport rates. Conditions will gradually be created which will spontaneously provide for the more rational distribution of production at the highest level of productivity.

In contrast to international cartels, which tend to impose restrictive practices on distribution and the exploitation of national markets, and to maintain high profits, the organization will ensure the fusion of markets and the expansion of production.

The essential principles and undertakings defined above will be the subject of a treaty signed between the States and submitted for the ratification of their parliaments. The negotiations required to settle details of applications will be undertaken with the help of an arbitrator appointed by common agreement. He will be entrusted with the task of seeing that the agreements reached conform with the principles laid down, and, in the event of a deadlock, he will decide what solution is to be adopted.

The common High Authority entrusted with the management of the scheme will be composed of independent persons appointed by the governments, giving equal representation. A chairman will be chosen by common agreement between the governments. The Authority's decisions will be enforceable in France, Germany and other member countries. Appropriate measures will be provided for means of appeal against the decisions of the Authority.

A representative of the United Nations will be accredited to the Authority, and will be instructed to make a public report to the United Nations twice yearly, giving an account of the working of the new organization, particularly as concerns the safeguarding of its objectives.

The institution of the High Authority will in no way prejudge the methods of ownership of enterprises. In the exercise of its functions, the common High Authority will take into account the powers conferred upon the International Ruhr Authority and the obligations of all kinds imposed upon Germany, so long as these remain in force.[44]

Paris, 9 May 1950

Bibliography

Books and reports

Fountain, Jeff. *Deeply Rooted: The Forgotten Legacy of Robert Schuman.* Heerde: The Schuman Centre for European Studies, 2010.
Kemper, R. Crosby. *Winston Churchill: Resolution, Defiance, Magnamity, Good Will.* Missouri: University of Missouri Press, 1996.
Mission and Public Affairs. *The Church of England and Europe Report."* London: Church of England, 2004.
Runcie, Robert. *Windows onto God.* London: SPCK, 1983.
Williams, Rowan. *Faith in the Public Square.* London: Bloomsbury, 2012.

Journal articles

European Parliament. "Regulation (EC) No 1717/2006 of the European Parliament and of the Council of 15 November 2006 Establishing an Instrument for Stability," *Official Journal of the European Union.* Accessed February 14, 2019. https://ec.europa.eu/fpi/sites/fpi/files/documents/regulation_1717_2006_15_11_2006_en.pdf.
European Parliament. "Regulation (EU) No 232/2014 of the European Parliament and of the Council of 11 March 2014 Establishing a European Neighbourhood Instrument,"

---

[44]   "The Schuman Declaration," accessed February 2, 2019, https://europa.eu/european-union/about-eu/symbols/europe-day/schuman-declaration_en.

Official Journal of the European Union. Accessed January 18, 2019. https://eur-lex. europa.eu/LexUriServ/LexUriServ.do?uri=OJ:L:2014:077:0027:0043:EN:PDF.

Websites

Andreani, Giles. "Europe's Uncertain Identity." Accessed February 20, 2019. https://www. cer.eu/sites/default/files/publications/attachments/pdf/2011/e_uncertain_identity-2215.pdf.

Archbishop of Canterbury. "Reconciliation." Accessed February 1, 2019. https://www. archbishopofcanterbury.org/priorities/reconciliation.

Archbishop of Canterbury. "Church must 'Look Outwards' to Tackle Climate Change, says Archbishop." Accessed February 20, 2019. https://www.archbishopofcanter bury.org/speaking-and-writing/speeches/church-must-look-outwards-tackle-climate-change-says-archbishop.

BBC News. "Full text: Blair's European Speech." Accessed February 19, 2019. http://news. bbc.co.uk/1/hi/uk_politics/4122288.stm.

CEC. "Conference of European Churches." Accessed February 27, 2013. http://www.ce ceurope.org/.

Coventry Cathedral. "Our Reconciliation Ministry." Accessed February 18, 2019. http:// www.coventrycathedral.org.uk/wpsite/our-reconciliation-ministry/?doing_wp_cron= 1550216269.1187551021575922773437.

COMECE. "The Catholic Church in the European Union." Accessed February 20, 2019. http://www.comece.org/.

European Commission. "The Treaty of Rome." Accessed February 1, 2019. https://ec.eu ropa.eu/romania/sites/romania/files/tratatul_de_la_roma.pdf.

European Commission. "Available Budget 2014–2020." Accessed February 19, 2019. http://ec.europa.eu/regional_policy/thefunds/funding/index_en.cfm.

European Council. "Final Declaration AU-EU Summit." Accessed February 1, 2019. https://www.consilium.europa.eu/media/31991/33454-pr-final_declaration_au_eu _summit.pdf.

European External Action Service. "The European Union at the United Nations, Fact Sheet." Accessed February 20, 2019. https://eeas.europa.eu/headquarters/head quarters-homepage/9875/european-union-united-nations_en.

European Union. "European Union Receives Nobel Peace Prize." Accessed February 18, 2019. https://europa.eu/european-union/about-eu/history/2010-today/2012/eu-no bel_en.

European Union. "Further Expansion." Accessed February 27, 2013. https://europa.eu/ european-union/about-eu/history/2000-2009_en.

European Union. "Living in the EU." Last modified December 20, 2018. http://europa.eu/ about-eu/facts-figures/living/index_en.htm.

European Union. "The Schuman Declaration – 9 May 1950." Accessed February 20, 2019. https://europa.eu/european-union/about-eu/symbols/europe-day/schuman-declara tion_en.

Hammond, Philip and David Davis. "Joint Article: A Deep and Special Partnership." Accessed January 18, 2019. https://www.gov.uk/government/news/joint-article-a-deep-and-special-partnership.

Maswana, Jean-Claude. "The Global Financial Crisis and Recession: Impact on and Development Prospects for Africa" Working Paper No. 15, 2010. Accessed February 19, 2019. https://www.jica.go.jp/jica-ri/publication/workingpaper/jrft3q00000022yl-att/JICA-RI_WP_No.15_2010.pdf.

NATO. "North Atlantic Treaty Organisation." Accessed February 27, 2013. http://www.nato.int/history/index.html.

Schuman Project. "Human Rights and the New Definition of Europe." Accessed February 27, 2019. http://users.belgacombusiness.net/schuman/HumanRights.htm.

Schuman Project. "Schuman Biography: Chronology." Accessed February 27, 2019. http://users.belgacombusiness.net/schuman/bio-details.htm.

Schuman Project. "The Definition of the New Europe." Accessed February 27, 2019. http://users.belgacombusiness.net/schuman/5May1949.htm.

St Ethelburga's Centre for Reconciliation and Peace. "About Our Work." Accessed February 18, 2019. https://stethelburgas.org/who-we-are/about-our-work/.

University of Birmingham. "It's the Slogan Stupid: The Brexit Referendum." Accessed February 1, 2019. https://www.birmingham.ac.uk/research/perspective/eu-ref-haughton.aspx.

II Context: European Societies and the Place of the Church

4. A Nation Divided against Itself?

Ben Ryan

We are witnessing a British public sphere that seems to be fracturing and becoming increasingly polarized. Brexit did not cause this polarization and fracturing, though it has gone some way to exacerbate some tensions, and has revealed others. Perhaps more importantly it has raised the stakes. A proper debate on the future of the UK's role in the world and key political and moral issues including migration policy, devolution and the status of the UK's constituent peoples and nations, economics and trade policy and others can no longer be avoided. These debates are not new, but the reality of Brexit has made reaching conclusions on the future an existential necessity. The status quo on an issue like immigration will change after Brexit, the only question is in what direction. There is an increased interest in the role of the Church in contributing to this fracturing, and what it might offer by way of solutions. This paper looks at three of the major dividing lines in British contemporary life and three means by which the Church can helpfully respond.

A caveat on Brexit and social divisions

There is a problem with viewing the question of whether there are serious social divisions in the UK through the lens of Brexit. The referendum was a binary choice, Leave or Remain, which lends itself to viewing two sides facing off across a chasm. In reality, the issues underpinning the referendum are so multi-faceted as to defy easy categorizations.

There have been various polls carried out to ask why people voted for Leave or Remain and the basic summary is that it was not one vote at all. True, a consistent feature of a number of polls of Leave voters has been that immigration has always been listed as either the most or second most important factor (most rank it top, but Lord Ashcroft's polls consistently had it second behind sovereignty).[1] However, others voted on the basis of sovereignty and control of laws, because we are thought to send too much money to the EU, because they were worried about the long-term trajectory of European integration and other issues. Conversely on the Remain side, the most common reason for voting was to do with economics, but also raised as concerns were the status of Northern Ireland, fears of becoming isolated on the world stage, the environment and other issues.

In other words, though the vote was, by nature, binary, the reality of the motivations behind the vote were much more complex. This is an important reminder when we use the data to try and draw big conclusions about a fractured public sphere. It is possible to correlate certain demographics with particular voting patterns, but it is important not to overclaim that such correlation indicates a necessarily high level of homogeneity in what those groups believe. Similarly, though it is an easy shorthand, it is dangerous to overgeneralize. There is no demographic that voted one hundred percent one way or the other (not even UKIP voters – four percent of whom voted Remain!),[2] and divisions within groups can be more painful and difficult than ones between groups. The isolation felt by someone who voted against their "tribe" can be severe – as a number of articles in the press have explored, including from an academic who felt they had been harassed by their colleagues for voting Leave, or another who described being a Brexit voter in Hampstead as "like coming out as gay in the 1950s."[3]

All those warnings aside, what we can say with some confidence is that the British public sphere is becoming increasing fractured and polarized, which can be seen (in an indicative sense if nothing more) in some of the divides revealed by the Brexit vote.

The dividing lines

There are a number of interesting factors to explore in terms of analysing the fracturing of the British public sphere but a few in particular stand out as factors worthy of further discussion for this forum:

---

[1]   See Lord Ashcroft, "How the United Kingdom Voted on Thursday… and Why," last modified June 24, 2016, https://lordashcroftpolls.com/2016/06/how-the-united-kingdom-voted-and-why/.

[2]   Ibid.

[3]   Quoted in Sarah Vine, "Voted Leave? It's One Way to Lose Friends," *The Spectator*, September 9, 2017, https://blogs.spectator.co.uk/2017/09/voted-leave-its-one-way-to-lose-friends-says-sarah-vine/.

- Age
- "Anywheres" and "Somewheres"
- Religious divides (both between religions and between denominations).

Age

Sixty-one percent of males aged 18 to 24 years voted for the UK to remain within the EU, whereas an equal 61 percent of males in the 50 to 64 age brackets voted in favour of Brexit. The peak share came from women between the ages of 18 and 24, 80 percent of whom voted for Remain (there's an interesting analysis to be done on gender voting patterns more broadly). Looking at age, there is a well-established narrative that young people voted Remain and older people voted Leave. More than 60 percent of all men over 50 voted leave, but the most Leave-backing group were women over 65, 66 percent of whom voted leave.

Those data tell a story, but do not necessarily do justice to some of the narratives at play, both before and after the vote. Anecdotally, on social media and in some newspaper columns the "blame" for what happened was put on older people, and there are many anecdotal accounts of family conflicts breaking out between generations. For a group of young people (though we need to be careful to remember that a significant minority still voted Brexit) the vote represented a failure of inter-generational solidarity, with older people having enjoyed the benefits of a system and then preventing their children and grandchildren from doing so. There were some very uncharitable suggestions that older people should not have been allowed a say, because ultimately this issue won't affect them in the future. Articles along those lines (some admittedly facetious or humorous) appeared in the *Guardian, Time, Forbes, Buzzfeed, Vice, The Independent, GQ magazine* and were widely discussed on social media.

This was a deeply unhelpful trend. It fed resentment among younger people who felt betrayed by their elders, while simultaneously disenfranchising older voters and dismissing their right to a democratic stake. It helped create a febrile atmosphere of intra-family conflict. It also put into sharp relief a wider point about inter-generational trends and conflicts. The youth are abandoning the mainstream political process. This is not a UK-specific phenomenon. In fact, it is arguably more striking on mainland Europe. In the most recent French presidential election a majority of the under-25 vote went to the extremes. More than 50 percent backed either the far-left candidate Jean-Luc Mélenchon, or the far right candidate Marine Le Pen.[4] We see similar trends in Germany, in the Netherlands, in Scandinavia and, increasingly, in the US.

The Oxford English Dictionary word of the year for 2017 was "Youthquake" – a significant cultural, political, or social change arising from the actions or influence of young people. The term was much used in the last British general election to explain the surprising results of the Labour share of the vote (in fact, it was subsequently largely debunked, but there was a feeling at the time that it was the youth vote which had been pivotal in driving the Labour result). This has been a long-term shift, the causes of which are various, but include the housing situation, the changing availability of credit, student debt, a mounting youth mental health crisis and various other factors. These have led to a string of books on the "jilted generation" – millennials who feel, with some justification, that baby boomers have asset-stripped the system, ignored the environment and national debt, and then left their children to pay for it.[5]

The diverging political interest of older and younger generations were shown up in the Brexit vote, but the polarization and divides between generations go much deeper than that vote alone might suggest. Of course, when it comes to the Church's contribution in this space it is worth noting that the young are also abandoning the Church. According to at least one recent survey only two percent of the British under-25s are members of the Church of England.[6]

"Anywheres" and "Somewheres"

"Anywheres" and "Somewheres" are the terms coined by the British political commentator David Goodhart in his 2017 book *The Road to Somewhere*.[7] Already the idea of the split between the two has become central to much political analysis. In Goodhart's model, "Anywheres" tend to be younger, university educated, urban, socially liberal (though, for Goodhart, often politically illiberal, cracking down on those not deemed to be sufficiently politically correct) and comfortable living anywhere without putting down deep roots in the community. Using British Social

---

[4]   See Joseph Bamat, "Mélenchon and Le Pen Win Over Youth in French Vote," *France 24,* April 24, 2017, https://www.france24.com/en/20170424-france-presidential-election-youth-vote-melenchon-le-pen.

[5]   See, for example, David Willets, *The Pinch: How the Baby Boomers Took Their Children's Future – And Why They Should Give It Back* (London: Atlantic Books, 2010).

[6]   See NatCen, "British Social Attitudes Survey, 35th Edition," accessed February 5, 2019, http://www.bsa.natcen.ac.uk/latest-report/british-social-attitudes-35/key-findings.aspx.

[7]   David Goodhart, *The Road to Somewhere: The Populist Revolt and the Future of Politics* (London: Hurst, 2017).

Attitudes data sets, he estimates they make up about 20 percent of the UK population. "Somewheres," by contrast, are rooted in a particular community, tend not to be university educated and though they are more socially liberal than is often imagined on many issues also hold other factors such as duty, nationhood and religion to be sacred. They make up about 50 percent of the population (the remainder fall into neither camp).

A number of commentators and political operatives have been persuaded that this divide has come to define the current malaise in British political life. Disproportionate, for Goodhart, attention has been paid to the politically dominant metropolitan elite class of "Anywheres" and their particular values. "Somewheres," by contrast have been largely ignored, or worse, actively disenfranchised. Brexit was in part a protest against this trend, and in part a reflection of genuine values of communities that were seeing rapid change and disruption to their values and way of life.

Central to the predicament of the "Somewheres" is that fear of a seemingly rapid and unstoppable change for which they never voted or opted into. Londoners may be confident in the cosmopolitanism and future of their city, but that is not a sentiment shared by many others. Indeed, one of the emerging splits that polling data continues to reveal is a growing divide between cities and towns. In fact, when it comes to attitudes to immigration, research has found that of the 100 areas where people were most likely to oppose immigration, all were in towns or on the outskirts of cities, with 93 of them in the Midlands or north of England. Conversely the 100 areas most linked with what the report calls the "confident multicultural" population were all in major cities or close to universities, with 90 percent of them within a few hundred metres of a university.[8]

We can overstate these concerns. There is significant polarization on immigration and on values more broadly between cosmopolitan cities and more "somewhere-y" towns. Research for the National Conversation on immigration hosted by British Futures found that most people in the UK have moderate views on migration, yet the debate is dominated by the louder voices at the fringes. Nevertheless, we can see some dividing lines at a values level that play out in differing community settings.

It is an interesting point to note that one of the single biggest predictors of votes for Brexit (and also for Donald Trump, for Victor Orbán and a host of populist right wing movements across Europe) is pessimism about the state of society. Those who believe that they "Don't recognize their country any more" are disproportionately likely to have backed Brexit (and to live in towns or rural areas). Similarly, the belief that things are worse now than they were twenty years

---

8   Rosie Carter, *Fear, Hope and Loss* (London: Hope Not Hate, 2018), accessed February 5, 2019, https://www.hopenothate.org.uk/wp-content/uploads/2018/10/FINAL-VERSION.pdf.

previously, and the expectation that things will get worse again, are again highly correlated with voting for Brexit. These are not niche views, but are held by up to 50 percent of the population according to some polls.[9]

Interestingly, though Brexit appealed to the pessimists, the success of the campaign was in promoting an optimistic vision for the future that appealed to that group that felt most distanced from the political programmes of the major parties over the past few decades. "Take back control" may not have necessarily had a lot of content behind it, but it did speak to a deep-seated desire to change the way things are. Similarly, Michael Gove's famous comment that we have "had enough of experts" was in a sense entirely true. The economic models and political promises of the past were never trusted and only tangentially seem to make a difference to people's lives; their appeal was minimal and Remain's failure to ever articulate a positive vision for the future seemed starkly at odds with the narratives and promises of a brash and energetic looking Leave campaign.

The success of this can be seen in recent polling by the organization "Hope not Hate", which finds that since the vote there has been, despite the well-documented difficulties in the negotiations, a surge of optimism among Leave supporters, who are now less likely than Remain supporters to describe themselves as pessimistic about the future, and much more likely to believe that Brexit will "increase economic opportunities for people like me."[10]

An interesting question for the Church in this scenario is quite where Christians sit in this "Anywhere"/"Somewhere" dichotomy. On the one hand churches are grounded in communities and, at least in principle, draw together people from a diverse range of ethnic, class, and educational backgrounds into a single gathered community sharing in a common identity. At the same time this is a community gathered for a goal that consciously transcends any local (or national) grounding. Churches exist in all communities with shared practices and beliefs (in the case of some with identical liturgies regardless of where in the country you might be), so someone can move from one part of the country to another and continue in their weekly worship in much the same way without great difficulty.

This question feeds into our next category of division: the differing trajectories of British religious groups.

Religious groups

There is always a difficulty in looking at religious polling in calculating what has been caused by religion and what is the result of other demographic factors. For example, we know that the average Anglican in the UK is older, and more likely to

---

[9]   See Ashcroft polling.

[10]   Carter, *Fear, Hope and Loss.*

live in towns and rural areas than the average British person. Since we also know that older people are more likely to back Leave, as are people in rural areas, how can we be sure that religion is the factor that made a difference?

Before coming to that, the headline figures do reveal some interesting distinctions between faith groups. Overall Muslims are the faith group who most overwhelmingly backed Remain (by 69 to 31 percent). They are also the youngest faith group and the most urban. Joining them in the Remain camp are other non-Christian groups (mostly Hindus and Sikhs, also an overwhelmingly urban group) by a 55:45 split and the non-religious (57:43 – this demographic tends to be younger). Catholics and Church of Scotland members voted slightly to Remain. On the Leave side by a very slight margin were Jews, and by a larger margin of 60:40 were Anglicans. Baptists and Methodists were split evenly.[11]

Other surveys have found different results. Linda Woodhead's Yougov exit poll found tighter margins across the board, except for Anglicans, who it suggested voted 66:34 for leave.[12] Catholics, in Woodhead's survey also voted by a small margin for Leave. If true this would be an exceptional result for Catholics, who, both historically and in other polls, have always been found to be slightly more pro-European than the British average.

Interestingly Woodhead's survey finds that church-attending Anglicans and Catholics are much more pro-European than those who call themselves Anglican or Catholic but do not attend church. In both cases there was a significant difference between the two groups. Church-attending Anglicans backed leave by 55:45, non-attending by 69:31; church-attending Catholics backed remain 59:41, non-attending backed Leave 56:44.

This may begin to reveal that religious identity and church attendance do have an impact even over and above other demographic trends. This bears out a long-standing academic tradition that has held that Catholics, across Europe, are significantly more pro-European than Protestants. Research by Nelson, Guth and Fraser has shown that Catholics tend to show greater support for EU integration and supranational solutions generally (and the more devout they are, the stronger their support tends to be).[13]

This is perhaps unsurprising, given the origins of the European project owe so much to a distinctively Catholic ideology. The term "Subsidiarity" in the European

---

[11] See Ben Clements, "How Religious Groups Voted in the 2016 Referendum on Britain's EU Membership," *British Religion in Numbers,* May 11, 2017, http://www.brin.ac.uk/how-religious-groups-voted-at-the-2016-referendum-on-britains-eu-membership/.

[12] See Greg Smith and Linda Woodhead, "Religion and Brexit: Populism and the Church of England," *Religion, State and Society,* 46 (2018): 206–223, doi: 10.1080/09637494.2018.1483861.

[13] See Brent Nelsen, James Guth, and Cleveland Fraser, "Does Religion Matter? Christianity and Public Support for the European Union," *European Union Politics* 2 (2001): 202.

treaties is explicitly drawn from Catholic Social Teaching. The great designers of the European project, Konrad Adenauer, Alcide De Gasperi, Jean Monnet, Robert Schuman and others, were Catholic, Christian Democrat politicians with a high view of supranational solutions to counter the evils of national politics (for which they blamed successive world wars). The European project was, in its origins, a Catholic ideological project.[14] It is accordingly little surprise that it prompts a greater degree of scepticism from those whose politics and identity are inspired by a more Protestant intellectual tradition. The Church of England and its adherents have tended to be closer to continental Protestants (particularly Scandinavians) than to Catholics when it comes to support for European integration.

While taking account of that, there is also a broader question about the relationship between Christian churches and the growth of populist right wing movements. On the whole the populist right in the UK has not had nearly the same success that it has had elsewhere in terms of instrumentalizing Christianity towards a nationalist agenda.

The sociologist Rogers Brubaker has characterized this wider European trend of instrumentalization as "a *Christianism*—not a substantive Christianity [...] It's a secularized Christianity as culture [...] It's a matter of belonging rather than believing." He furthers describes the attitude as being one in which "*We* are Christians precisely because *they* are Muslims. Otherwise, we are not Christian in any substantive sense."[15]

This is a trend that has been apparent in various European countries. After decades in which the German CSU party was criticized for losing its religion and suppressing its Christian origins suddenly, and to its critics only as a means of heading off election losses to the far right, its leaders have been campaigning for the introduction of crucifixes into public schools in Bavaria. It is a tactic which has been seen in anti-establishment right-wing parties in a number of countries. In Italy *Lega Nord* (usually known in English as "The League"), a right-wing populist party, has campaigned for crucifixes to be obligatory in all public buildings, including schools, ports and prisons. Matteo Salvini, the deputy prime minister of Italy and the party's leader has made a point (despite vociferous criticism from the Church) of holding a rosary during speeches. Salvini does, it seems, attend mass (though he was publicly a neo-pagan for many years), but his party's record on relationships with the Church (in common with a number of populist parties) is a curious one, oscillating between rampant anti-clericalism and claims to Catholic authenticity.

---

[14]   For more detail see Ben Ryan, *A Soul for the Union* (London: Theos, 2015).

[15]   Quoted by Emma Green, "The Specter of Catholic Identity in Secular France," *The Atlantic*, May 6, 2017, https://www.theatlantic.com/international/archive/2017/05/christian-identity-france/525558/.

The story repeats itself across Europe, with parties including the German *Alternative für Deutschland* party (Alternative for Germany), who have referred to their role as to defend the "western Christian culture."[16] These would include the Dutch PVV (*Partij voor de Vrijheid* – Party for Freedom), the Flemish *Vlaams Belang* (Flemish Interest), and a number of parties in Poland, Hungary, Slovakia and elsewhere who have all at one point or another laid claim to being the party of Christian values, particularly in opposition to Islam.

And yet, despite all the evidence of the instrumentalization of religion by right-wing populists, the other side of the coin is that religion seems to provide an "immunization" against right-wing populist politics. There are several aspects to this. In countries with functional Christian political parties, church-going Christians do not tend to abandon those parties and so are simply not available to the far right. This would apply, for example, in the Netherlands, Belgium, Germany and Scandinavia. In those countries, church going serves as an inoculation against the tendency to vote for the populist right. Statistically this effect is significant: active Christians are disproportionately likely in such countries to resist the overtures of the far right. In those countries where there are no Christian political parties (e.g. the USA, UK), the effect is significantly reduced, or even, by some estimates, non-existent.[17]

Much also depends on the particular history of religion and its association with the national culture in question. In countries in which religion is closely associated with national identity (e.g. Lutheranism in Scandinavia or Catholicism in Italy), there is some evidence that the right-wing populists can tap into religious identity to gain support (though again, actually going to church seems to reduce that effect). However, if particular Christian denominations are not associated with national identity then religion can act as a really significant barrier to support for nationalist policies. Catholicism, for example, while it can be used in Italy to support nationalist parties, serves as a major block to the same trend in countries like the USA, Germany and the UK where it has little association with historic notions of national identity.

Finally, and crucially, the actual role of churches has a significant effect. Where churches have been public and vocal in their opposition to right wing populism (e.g. France and Germany where the churches have been vociferous in

---

[16]   "Manifesto for Germany: The Political Programme of the Alternative for Germany," accessed February 8, 2019, https://www.afd.de/wp-content/uploads/sites/111/2017/04/2017-04-12_afd-grundsatzprogramm-englisch_web.pdf.

[17]   See Kai Arzheimer and Elisabeth Carter, "Christian Religiosity and Voting for West European Radical Right Parties," *West European Politics*, 32 (2009): 985–1011, doi: 10.1080/01402380903065058; and Tim Immerzeel, Eva Jaspers and Marcel Lubbers, "Religion as Catalyst or Restraint of Radical Right Voting?," *West European Politics*, 36 (2013): 946–968, doi: 10.1080/01402382.2013.797235.

their criticism of right-wing populist groups) church attendance is strongly correlated with not voting for such parties. Indeed, in countries where churches have been vocal in opposition that effect seems to extend even to non-practicing Christians.[18] Moreover, vocal church opposition can lead to right-wing populists being more reticent about attempting to instrumentalize religion in the first instance. A few sporadic efforts aside the UK's foremost populist right-wing party, UKIP, have made little systematic effort to position themselves as the party of Christian values, and it is theorized that this may be linked to the fact that the Church of England and Catholic Church in England and Wales have both been prominent and consistent in their support for refugees and sympathy towards migrants more generally.[19]

Beyond the dividing lines

The above section analysed some of the dividing lines (there are plenty of others) that seem to be characterizing an increasingly fractured British public sphere. This presents a serious problem for doing politics and public life. Jürgen Habermas's vision of a public square rests on there being a meaningful shared language and set of values that unites the *demos.* We seem to be losing that basis for unity. In an increasingly tribalized and polarized space, the perceived normal rules of politics are breaking down. The inevitable follow up has to be whether there is anything the Church can usefully provide to aid with this situation.

One answer which is given frequently is that churches by their nature provide a means of overcoming some of these divisions. We are, as Robert Putnam and others have demonstrated, a society that is losing community hubs.[20] There are fewer and fewer well attended institutional settings in which people from different backgrounds ever come into contact with one another. Churches are increasingly unusual in hosting people of different ages, economic groups and racial and ethnic backgrounds. There is certainly a deal of truth to this. It is, of course, rather undermined by the fact that church membership, like every other institution is also declining, particularly among younger generations. In 2017 more than half

---

[18]   See Nadia Marzouki, Duncan McDonnell, and Oliver Roy (eds.), *Saving the People: How Populists Hijack Religion* (London: Hurst & Company, 2016).

[19]   See Timothy Peace, "Religion and Populism in Britain," in: *Saving the People: How Populists Hijack Religion*, edited by Nadia Marzouki, Duncan McDonnel and Oliver Roy. London: Hurst, 2016; and Steven Woodbridge, "Christian Credentials?: The Role of Religion in British National Party Ideology," *Journal for the Study of Radicalism*, 4 (2010): 25–54, doi 10.1353/jsr.0.0039.

[20]   See Robert Putnam, *Bowling Alone: The Collapse and Revival of American Community* (New York: Simon & Schuster, 2000).

of the British population described themselves as having no religion for the first time.

Nevertheless, there are three major areas to which the Church might contribute something to our current situation:

- Practical (community building and resilience)
- Advocacy
- Vision and values.

Practical

Regardless of whether church congregations are shrinking or not there is a critical role to be played by the church as an institution in building local communities and supporting social resilience. Research from Theos over the past few years has revealed the often critical role played by churches in supporting areas with high levels of multiple deprivation.[21] Recent research, for instance, has looked at the role of churches in the North East in building community resilience,[22] and at the faith response to the Grenfell Tower disaster.[23]

This is underpinned further by the provision of spaces in which communities can gather. A key finding of a series of our reports at Theos think tank, a British think tank specializing in research into religion and society, has been the importance of physical presence – the church building itself – being able to provide a hub for the community.

There are a number of factors that underpin successful church work on these issues – including presence, being constantly *in* a place, with the time to work beside people. Most other agencies and charities come and go, so part of the appeal of church groups is their constant presence and commitment to a place regardless of the priorities of government or the charity sector. The longevity and true presence within communities differentiates faith groups from most other actors.

If communities are going to fracture and divide, the building blocks for resolving that situation must in part be practical. Research carried out on effective multiculturalism, and the work done by community organizers, suggests that the best means of building trust between groups is through common endeavours on issues

---

[21] See Paul Bickley, *Good Neighbours: How Churches Help Communities to Flourish* (London: Church Urban Fund and Theos, 2014).

[22] See Paul Bickley, *People, Place and Purpose: Churches and Neighbourhood Resilience in the North East* (London: Theos, 2018).

[23] See Amy Plender, *After Grenfell: The Faith Groups' Response* (London: Theos, 2018).

that transcend difference.[24] In this the Church has a critical role to play both in continuing its current community social action work, and in ensuring that such work in the future is ever more effective, despite the difficulties in shrinking congregations and the challenges of the current economic situation.

Advocacy

The Church of England and others have a political presence and ability to advocate for various causes. The Church of England has been effective in its lobbying and campaigning for the rights of asylum seekers, and in leading efforts at community resettlement. Its efforts at lobbying and leading in that space have helped to counteract the appeal of the far right and to lend prominence to the issue in public debate. Arguably, the Church of England has had rather less success in differentiating itself from the campaigning priorities of the political left, despite the fact that the majority of self-identifying Anglicans tend to vote conservative. It has been suggested that this leads to a degree of disconnect between the Church's leadership and the pews.[25]

That said, the consistent condemnation of the Church of England (and other churches) of the far right and anti-immigrant rhetoric has been examined as a key factor in the relative impotence of the far right in Britain. Whereas in much of Europe Christianity has been co-opted by right-wing movements, that effect has been relatively limited in the UK, an effect which can largely be ascribed to the public condemnation of such ideas by the Church of England.[26]

There is some consensus that religious interventions in public debate can be effective more broadly. The profile and status of the Church of England as the established Church gives it a particular platform from which to advocate for particular causes. In the particular climate of fracturing and polarization it is not necessarily clear what advocacy roles the Church can play most helpfully. Certainly, the continued work around migrant groups, especially asylum seekers, will continue to be helpful. It is a more difficult question to consider what the Church might do to build bridges between age groups and between other faiths.

One opportunity presented by the Brexit vote is the chance for the Church to play an instrumental role in advocating for future international political models.

---

[24] See David Barclay, *Making Multiculturalism Work: Enabling practical action across deep difference* (London: Theos, 2013).

[25] See Linda Woodhead, "CofE Clergy Concerned with Protecting the Welfare Budget," Lancaster University Website, October 24, 2014, https://www.lancaster.ac.uk/news/articles/2014/cofe-clergy-concerned-with-protecting-the-welfare-budget/.

[26] See Peace, "Religion and Populism in Britain," and Woodbridge, "Christian Credentials?," 25–54.

The Brexit debate was characterized by an unhealthy consensus on both sides that everything in international politics was either to be credited to, or blamed on, the EU. The Remain side were often insufficiently critical of an EU which does exhibit serious flaws in both design and practice. The Leave side were insufficiently mindful of those good things that the EU provides in terms of international solutions to major issues, including climate change and international security. Certainly the UK, in a globalized economy, and facing international challenges including terrorism, a global migration crisis and the environment, cannot afford to become an isolated pariah state. That does not mean that the EU is necessarily the right answer to all these challenges. The opportunity for the Church is to hold politics to account and to shape future collaborations in this space. There is plenty of history for this. The European project itself was greatly shaped by the contribution of Catholic intellectuals and movements. The UN Declaration of Human Rights came about in part due to the work of the World Council of Churches. Both of these were twentieth-century achievements shaped by their own context. There is a major advocacy task for the Church to identify, encourage and shape future international collaborations.

Vision and values

In 2014 the then British prime minister David Cameron declared that he considered the UK to be a "Christian country".[27] This provoked an immediate response from a list (gathered by the British Humanist Association) of academics and celebrities who wrote a letter to *The Telegraph* in which they said that they:

> ...object to his [Cameron's] characterisation of Britain as a "Christian country" and the negative consequences for politics and society that this engenders [...] At a social level, Britain has been shaped for the better by many pre-Christian, non-Christian, and post-Christian forces. We are a plural society with citizens with a range of perspectives, and we are a largely non-religious society.[28]

Such complaints are deliberately obtuse. While it is obviously true that the UK population is not now (nor ever has been) universally Christian (as we saw above) and, equally obviously, that there was a world before Christianity in what is now

---

[27] From a speech at the Downing Street Easter reception, April 2014, accessed February 27, 2019, https://www.gov.uk/government/speeches/easter-reception-at-downing-street-2014.

[28] Letter to the *Daily Telegraph* "David Cameron Fosters Division by Calling Britain a 'Christian' Country," April 20, 2014, https://www.telegraph.co.uk/comment/letters/10777417/David-Cameron-fosters-division-by-calling-Britain-a-Christian-country.html.

the UK, the idea that that makes Christianity just one influence among many is clearly nonsense. Culturally, legally, philosophically, the UK and the West has been forged in a distinctively Christian milieu, and is defined by that milieu.

This truth is often denied or forgotten in public debate. The vision of a common public with a shared language and values demands a conscious appreciation of the heritage that binds us. It is difficult to find a collective vision for the future without having a consensus on the ties that bind us. There is a role here for the Church which is more prophetic: to continue to proclaim the basis of Western culture.

To recognize that is not Christian over-claiming; it is simply a recognition of who we are and what has shaped our intellectual horizons. Or as Jean-Paul Sartre (famously no fan of Christianity) was to observe:

> [...] we are all still Christians today; the most radical unbelief is Christian atheism, an atheism that despite its destructive power preserves guiding schemes – very few for thought, more for the imagination, most for the sensibility, whose source lies in the centuries of Christianity to which we are heirs, like it or not.[29]

Building that intellectual case for a shared community based on common values is an essential task of intellectual evangelism for the British churches.

Concluding challenge: soul politics

One of the responses I received to a version of this paper given at Lambeth Palace was a challenge around the role of patriotism. Amid media discussion of the role of economics, the so-called "left behinds", accusations of electoral malpractice, foreign interference and a host of other factors to explain the vote, there has been relatively little appreciation for the extent to which the Leave campaign resonates with people's sense of British identity and pride. The Church of England, oddly for a national church, has often seemed to struggle to articulate a positive vision of national identity as relates to politics. The divide between a Leave campaign that tapped into patriotic pride and a national church that seems to struggle to do so (and which, at least among its bishops, seemed to overwhelmingly back remaining in the EU) is a striking and worrying feature.

This is related to a broader problem in British (and European) public life. In the section on dividing lines above I referred to David Goodhart's distinction between "Anywheres" and "Somewheres" as a key societal division. However, I think that that divide can be taken further, and perhaps we need to think more

---

[29]   Jean-Paul Sartre, *The Family Idiot*, translated Carol Cosman, (Chicago: Chicago University Press, 1991), vol 4, 346.

about a divide between "mind" and "soul" as a means of belonging. In this schema, mind-based visions of belonging hinge on rational choices. Identity is a considered choice of pros and cons; an opted-into identity. By contrast soul-based visions of belonging are simply intrinsic; they are a matter of what someone fundamentally *is* and cannot be otherwise.

The Brexit referendum, the Church response and much of contemporary politics is breaking down along these lines. A feature of the Remain campaign was the appeal to the mind-belonging vision. Voters were encouraged to vote in their economic best interests and a practical, rational and rights-based vision. The Leave campaign appealed to soul-belonging. Their pitch was something more visceral and intrinsic; an appeal to the truth of what it meant to be British, and to be proud of that. It legitimized and empowered a sense of people's deeper identity.

Too much of contemporary politics, including the advocacy of the churches, is losing the soul battle. The interventions of the Church of England around Brexit have, on the whole, given no succour to a deeper sense of identity and belonging. In many ways their interventions have been indistinguishable from many well-meaning secular charities and campaign groups. As we look to the future this needs to change. We need to continue the practical, advocacy and visionary role of the Church in society, but in doing so there is a fundamental call to do so from a soulful perspective: to ensure that the interventions really do appeal to the deepest spiritual level of our citizens.

Bibliography

Books and reports

Barclay, David. *Making Multiculturalism Work: Enabling Practical Action Across Deep Difference.* London: Theos, 2013.

Bickley, Paul. *Good Neighbours: How Churches Help Communities to Flourish.* London: Church Urban Fund and Theos, 2014.

Bickley, Paul. *People, Place and Purpose: Churches and Neighbourhood Resilience in the North East.* London: Theos, 2018.

Carter, Rosie. *Fear, Hope and Loss.* London: Hope Not Hate, 2018.

Goodhart, David. *The Road to Somewhere: The Populist Revolt and the Future of Politics.* London: Hurst, 2017.

Marzouki N., McDonnell D., Roy O. (eds). *Saving the People: How Populists Hijack Religion.* London: Hurst, 2016.

Plender, Amy. *After Grenfell: the Faith Groups' Response.* London: Theos, 2018.

Putnam, Robert. *Bowling Alone: The Collapse and Revival of American Community.* New York: Simon & Schuster, 2000.

Ryan, Ben. *A Soul for the Union.* London: Theos, 2015.

Sartre, Jean-Paul. *The Family Idiot*, translated Carol Cosman, vol 4. Chicago: Chicago University Press, 1991.

Willets, David. *The Pinch: How the Baby Boomers Took Their Children's Future – And Why They Should Give It Back.* London: Atlantic Books, 2010.

Journal articles

Arzheimer, Kai, and Elisabeth Carter. "Christian Religiosity and Voting for West European Radical Right Parties." *West European Politics* 32 (2009): 985–1011. doi: 10.1080/01402380903065058.

Immerzeel, Tim, Eva Jaspers and Marcel Lubbers. "Religion as Catalyst or Restraint of Radical Right Voting?" *West European Politics* 36 (2013): 946–968. doi: 10.1080/01402382.2013.797235.

Nelsen, Brent, James Guth, and Cleveland Fraser. "Does Religion Matter? Christianity and Public Support for the European Union" *European Union Politics* 2 (2001): 191–217.

Smith, Greg and Linda Woodhead. "Religion and Brexit: Populism and the Church of England." *Religion, State and Society* 46 (2018): 206–223. doi: 10.1080/09637494.2018.1483861.

Woodbridge, Steven. "Christian Credentials?: The Role of Religion in British National Party Ideology". *Journal for the Study of Radicalism* 4 (2010): 25–54. doi: 10.1353/jsr.0.0039.

Websites

Lord Ashcroft Polls. "How the United Kingdom Voted on Thursday… and Why." Accessed January 8, 2019. https://lordashcroftpolls.com/2016/06/how-the-united-kingdom-voted-and-why/.

Clements, Ben. "How Religious Groups Voted in the 2016 Referendum on Britain's EU Membership" *British Religion in Numbers.* Accessed January 8, 2019. http://www.brin.ac.uk/how-religious-groups-voted-at-the-2016-referendum-on-britains-eu-membership/.

Woodhead, Linda. "CofE Clergy Concerned with Protecting the Welfare Budget." Accessed January 8, 2019. https://www.lancaster.ac.uk/news/articles/2014/cofe-clergy-concerned-with-protecting-the-welfare-budget/.

AFD "Manifesto for Germany: The Political Programme of the Alternative for Germany." https://www.afd.de/wp-content/uploads/sites/111/2017/04/2017-04-12_afd-grundsatz programm-englisch_web.pdf.

Press articles

Bamat, Joseph. "Mélenchon and Le Pen Win Over Youth in French Vote" *France 24* April 24, 2017. https://www.france24.com/en/20170424-france-presidential-election-youth-vote-melenchon-le-pen.

Letter to the *Daily Telegraph* "David Cameron Fosters Division by Calling Britain a 'Christian country.'" April 20, 2014. https://www.telegraph.co.uk/comment/letters/10777417/David-Cameron-fosters-division-by-calling-Britain-a-Christian-country.html.

Green, Emma. "The Specter of Catholic Identity in Secular France." *The Atlantic,* May 6, 2017. https://www.theatlantic.com/international/archive/2017/05/christian-identity-france/525558/.

Vine, Sarah. "Voted Leave? It's One Way to Lose Friends." *The Spectator,* September 9, 2017. https://blogs.spectator.co.uk/2017/09/voted-leave-its-one-way-to-lose-friends-says-sarah-vine/.

5. Social Divisions Associated with Brexit: How Are they Replicated in Other European Countries, and How Are Churches Responding to them?

Arnulf von Scheliha

I. Introduction: diagnosis of social divisions

It is obvious that the mental and social conditions that may have contributed to the victory of Brexit supporters in the British referendum in June 2016 are not transferable to or replicated in Germany. After the Second World War, Germany had a very specific position in Europe. For Germany, the process of European unification was an opportunity to establish and stabilize democracy, increase economic success, reconstruct the country, and seek reconciliation with the former arch enemy, France.

The churches supported these developments. The idea of European unification was inspired to a significant extent by Roman Catholic thinkers such as Jacques Maritain (1882–1973), and by liberal socialists such as Altiero Spinelli (1907–1986), Ernesto Rossi (1897–1967) and Eugenio Colorni (1909–1933). Konrad Adenauer (1876–1967), Alcide de Gasperi (1881–1954) and Robert Schuman (1886–1963) were Roman Catholic statesmen who realized the European idea politically. The Protestant churches in Germany were somewhat more sceptical towards the Western orientation of Adenauer's politics, because they long saw themselves as an institution of German unity. Despite the division of Germany, the Evangelical Church in Germany (EKD) remained as a union of regional churches in both parts of Germany until 1969. Only in that year was the Confederation of Evangelical Churches founded as a union of the eight regional churches in the GDR.[1] In 1985, in its well-known memorandum, the EKD made a commitment to democracy and the rule of law, combining human rights and the concept of human dignity with the Christian notion of the image of God in the human being, and encouraging Christian responsibility for political participation and

---

[1] See Claudia Lepp and Kurt Nowak, ed., *Evangelische Kirche im geteilten Deutschland (1945–1989/90)* (Göttingen: Vandenhoeck & Ruprecht, 2001).

social justice.[2] But it does not mention European institutions or European development, which were on the increase at that time. That was made up for after German unification in 1990.[3] Today, the EKD defends "the free, social, economic and moral achievements of Europe" against the "threat from populist and extremists, and also from dwindling support in the member states".[4]

On the whole, the process of European unification offered Germans the chance of rehabilitation by the international world after the dark period of German history. This is well-known in our country, so European scepticism is not widespread in Germany. Of course, there is some uneasiness with European bureaucracy and some complaints about opaque rulings made in "Brussels". But there is no significant social force that is questioning Germany's membership of the EU. The new party "Alternative für Deutschland" (AfD), which is now the largest opposition party in the German parliament, began as a counter movement to the Euro and to the policies adopted to stabilize the common currency during the financial crisis of 2008. Today, the party manifesto states that the party "is in favour of returning the European Union to an economic union based on shared interests and consisting of sovereign, but loosely connected, national states". It is only if reform of the EU does not succeed that "we shall seek Germany's exit, or a democratic dissolution of the EU".[5] This party wants to strengthen national states and the rule of German law, but is distant from the radicalism of EU-opponents in England, France, Italy and the Netherlands, for example.

---

[2]   See EKD, *Evangelische Kirche und freiheitliche Demokratie. Der Staat des Grundgesetzes als Angebot und Aufgabe. Eine Denkschrift der Evangelischen Kirche in Deutschland* (Gütersloh: Gütersloher Verlagshaus, 1985); and Hans Michael Heinig, ed., *Aneignung des Gegebenen. Entstehung und Wirkung der Demokratie-Denkschrift der EKD* (Tübingen: Mohr Siebeck, 2017).

[3]   See, for example, the joint text issued by the Council of the Evangelical Church in Germany (EKD) and the German (Roman Catholic) Bishops' Conference "Demokratie braucht Tugenden": Rat der Evangelische Kirche in Deutschland and Katholische Kirche Deutsche Bischofskonferenz, *Demokratie braucht Tugenden. Gemeinsames Wort des Rates der Evangelischen Kirche in Deutschland und der Deutschen Bischofskonferenz zur Zukunft unseres demokratischen Gemeinwesens* (Hannover: Kirchenamt der Evangelischen Kirche in Deutschland and Bonn: Sekretariat der Deutschen Bischofskonferenz, 2006), 12.

[4]   EKD, "Statement by the Council of the Evangelical Church in Germany (EKD) on the situation of Europe, Brussels, 23 April 2016," 1, accessed February 20, 2019, https://www.ekd.de/ekd_en/ds_doc/20160423_erklaerung_zur_lage_europas_en.pdf.

[5]   AfD, "Grundsatzprogramm," 15, accessed February 20, 2019, https://www.afd.de/grundsatzprogramm/. See also the manifesto for the elections to the European Parliament 2019: AfD, "DEXIT – The Exit as Last Option," 15, accessed February 20, 2019, https://www.afd.de/wp-content/uploads/sites/111/2019/02/AfD_Euro pawahlprogramm_A5-hoch_web.pdf.

Nevertheless, the financial and refugee crises since 2014 have created the feeling of social divisions in Germany as well. It is sometimes combined with another feeling of social division that we call "the wall in people's heads" ("Mauer in den Köpfen"), which is a replication of the former border between the GDR and West Germany. This phrase symbolizes the fact that there are people who "lost out" socially and economically as a result of German unification, and who criticize the established institutions of the "old West Germany". This division intensifies debates on social justice, on the noticeable gap between urban and rural areas, and on the fear of the increasing visibility of Islam in Germany. Politics is not picking up on all these social divisions at the moment, because these problems have long been concealed by a positive economic situation. Furthermore, Angela Merkel's long period of chancellorship in grand coalitions has absorbed an influential and strong parliamentary opposition, and the creativity to identify and solve problems. But the problems are now becoming more apparent. The established parties are losing people's trust and the current German government lacks stability. It is staggering from crisis to crisis, and we expect the coalition to end at any time. Against this backdrop, the European achievements of Germany recede into the background.

To sum up: there is a special form of social division in Germany; there is not a demand to leave the EU, but rather a growing mistrust in established institutions and parties; it is this mistrust that politics and churches have to react to.

If churches understand themselves as institutions that stand in the middle of society and that have something to offer all people, then their main task would be to initiate social debates so as to reconcile social divisions and to moderate them locally and regionally. But, beyond this moderating function, churches can also (II) propagate the idea of political cooperation in Europe and European values, (III) make their own contributions to constructing a liberal and tolerant culture of religion in plurality, and (IV) mitigate the cost of social divisions caused by modern life and migration.

II. Speaking up for the European period of peace

The main point that European churches should stress in speaking up for the European idea is the long period of peace in Europe. We have to recall that such periods of peace are very rare in European history.[6] From the perspective of the ethics of peace, the European unification and political collaboration established after the Second World War is a moral achievement of the utmost importance. Europe as a

---

[6]   Some church statements on Europe create the misunderstanding that peace is one achievement among many. But this underestimates the fundamental significance of peace and cooperation free of violence (see, for example: "Statement by the Council").

peace project is the answer not only to dictatorship and both world wars, but also to the European wars of the long nineteenth century with their overheated nationalism. Its importance is comparable to the Peace of Westphalia.

The treaty negotiated and agreed upon in the cities of Osnabrück and Münster in 1648 brought to an end the Thirty Years' War between religious enemies. The Westphalian system of sovereign nations was founded, with the well-known formula *cuius regio eius religio* prescribing that there be only *one* religion in *one* state, and that the feudal government decides which religion is established in its domain. On this basis, a pluralistic culture of religion evolved in Europe, one that included Roman Catholic, Lutheran, Calvinist, and Anglican Christians, and in the long run Jewish communities as well. Under the rule of law guaranteed by a strong government, religions learnt to respect the neutrality of law as an important instrument for resolving religious conflicts. Governments learnt to respect religion since religious minorities were given the right to migrate if their faith was not recognized in their country.

The European institutions established after the Second World War have now created in central Europe a space for peace that has endured for 70 years. Given the history of Europe, that is a period of time without precedence. Close economic links, measures of reconciliation and understanding between European people and political institutions were the moral answer to the disaster of intensified nationalism in European states – and in German Protestantism. The force of attraction of the European peace-building process after the Second World War became clear after 1989 when the states of the former Warsaw pact joined the EU, followed 10 years later by the Balkan states, which had been at war during the 1990s.

Again, Christian churches have benefitted greatly from this European peace, which has made possible for the first time an ecumenical understanding between the Christian confessions. I mention as examples the Second Vatican Council (1962–1965) with its approach to Christian ecumenism and interreligious dialogue, the Leuenberg Agreement (1973), the Meissen Declaration (1988), and the Conference of European Churches (CEC). It is no coincidence that during this process of European peace-building, important Christian churches learnt to acknowledge and to adopt the tradition of human rights and human dignity, and to combine it with the Biblical tradition of the image of God in the human being. This is precisely what the Roman Catholic Church did during the Second Vatican Council. In 1985, the German churches and theology summarized their history of learning in the memorandum that I have mentioned above.[7]

Europe as a space of peace is the basis for mitigating social divisions and realizing social justice. This basis should be emphasized by churches as a high moral

---

[7]   See Arnulf von Scheliha, "Politik im neutralen, säkularen Staat – Wie reagier(t)en die Religionen?" *Bibel und Liturgie ... in kulturellen Räumen* 90 (2017).

good. And this very significant achievement can be emphasized as a way of countering the mistrust in European bureaucracy and its long-winded procedures, because Europe as a space of peace is more than the EU, and contains other important institutions that deal with social conflicts and peace-building, such as the "Council of Europe" (CoE) and the "Organization for Security and Co-operation in Europe" (OSCE). Especially the European Convention on Human Rights (ECHR) and the European Court of Human Rights (ECtHR) are highly important institutions in furthering the process of peace-building in Europe including the United Kingdom.

But, in focusing on peace and human rights, churches have to remember that, from a historical perspective, the first steps to building peace in Europe were *economic* integration and the *rule of private law*. The process began when the European Economic Community (EEC) was created by the Treaty of Rome in 1957. The common market formed the basis for the political integration that gradually followed. The Schengen Agreement and the introduction of a common currency are measures to achieve more freedom within the sphere of *civil society*. But theology and the churches tend to overlook this special starting position of European development and peace-building,[8] perhaps because German churches especially cultivate an anti-capitalist perspective that is focused on public law as an instrument to restrict market freedom. So, in my opinion, the Christian churches need a broader concept of the ethics of peace, one that includes economic freedom at the same level as social justice and cultural responsibility. We must not underestimate the important contribution that economic interdependence makes to understanding between peoples. To put it more generally: in propagating the idea of European peace, churches should not only address the European institutions and public law, but also focus on civil society and the responsibility of individuals which includes social justice and fairness. In this field we have to do both; to support the forces seeking to protect and broaden the spheres of freedom, and to consider the interests of those people who bear the costs of freedom.

III. Establishing a European culture of religion in plurality

In his contribution to this volume, Piers Ludlow analyses the silent but important role of Christianity in the integration process, and he convincingly noted the

---

[8]   See, for example, the joint statement by the Chair of the Council of the Evangelical Church in Germany (EKD) and the Chair of the German (Roman Catholic) Bishops' Conference marking the 60th anniversary of the signing of the Rome Treaties: EKD, "We continue to pin our hopes on Europe", accessed February 20, 2019, https://www.ekd.de/ekd_en/ds_doc/ecumenical_statement_of_signing_of_rome_treaties.pdf.

reasons for the long-time "veil of silence around the question of religion".[9] But in these days the silence is broken. The European culture of religion is becoming increasingly pluralistic. Many people feel threatened by Islam and Judaism. This could increase social divisions. How should churches react? Roman Catholic theology and the Roman Catholic Church suggest the idea of a "Christian Europe" as a model for the world, the idea of a Europe that cultivates hospitality to other religions.[10] At first glance, this seems to be a positive suggestion. But I do not think that it takes the pluralistic situation seriously enough. I would like to suggest referring instead to Ernst Troeltsch's concept of a "European cultural synthesis" (Europäische Kultursynthese), which I would now like to outline.

From a Protestant perspective, the theologian and philosopher Ernst Troeltsch (1865–1923) provided the most important contribution to understanding the idea of Europe historically.[11] His main historiographical concept is "cultural synthesis", which allows us to integrate complex and contrary movements in describing European identity. How does it work? Troeltsch starts off with the thesis that Europe is a mixture of ancient and modern worlds.[12] He identifies within the ancient world three "fundamental forces" that played an important role during the process of becoming Europe. Troeltsch mentions Hebraic prophecy, classical Greek antiquity, and ancient imperialism. The latter is characterized by two features – namely, the world power realized in the Roman Empire based on bureaucracy and the military on the one hand, and the world religion of Christianity on the other. An additional "fundamental force" became important during the Occidental medieval period, and this was driven by the church.

> It is the result of the self-decomposition of antiquity, the salvation of the state, culture and society in the church formation of society, and the relative restoration of antiquity through just this church, that made possible in the Byzantine Empire a new formation of the ancient Roman state and the transference of this and its culture in the Germanic-Romanic peoples to the new barbarian peoples and changed them according to their needs. This is the tremendous, world-historical significance of the Christian churches for our culture.[13]

---

[9]   Piers Ludlow, "Silent but Important: Religion as a Factor in the Integration Process," 40 above.

[10] See Arnulf von Scheliha, *Protestantische Ethik des Politischen* (Tübingen: Mohr Siebeck, 2013), 250–253.

[11] Troeltsch called it "Europaism;" see Ernst Troeltsch, *Der Historismus und seine Probleme* (Gesammelte Schriften III) (Tübingen: Mohr, 1922), 703 ff.

[12] Troeltsch, *Historismus*, 716.

[13] "Sie ist das Ergebnis der Selbstzersetzung der Antike, die Rettung von Staat, Kultur und Gesellschaft in die kirchliche Gesellschaftsbildung und die relative Wiederherstellung der Antike durch eben diese Kirche, die im byzantinischen Reich eine Neubildung des antiken Römerstaates möglich machte und in den germanisch-romanischen Völkern die-

The *modern* world emerges by emancipating cultural spheres from affiliation to church life. Since the Enlightenment period, the rational principles of culture have ruled the European spirit. The rational ethics of humanity, research in the natural sciences, ideologies and historical consciousness emerged. "The European world lives its life" according to these general principles of culture.[14] For Troeltsch, churches played primarily a role of transition by achieving the European synthesis of culture.[15]

Troeltsch emphasized the essential aspects of European culture. Rational secularity and historical consciousness certainly belong to the main features of European identity. Christianity is embedded in specific contrary movements in Europe. The church was dominant in the medieval period, but important cultural achievements of this age were connected with intolerance and the oppression of minorities and dissenters. The Reformation provided essential impulses for establishing freedom and tolerance. But, due to the close relationship between state and church in Protestant countries, political freedom and social emancipation had to be imposed against the will of churches and their theologies.

In describing the role of Christianity and churches in Europe, we have to notice their important historical contributions, but also their embeddedness in conflicts with rational ideas, sciences and values. Today the values that create modern Europe could be interpreted as an expression of Christianity according to this history of learning and the adoption of rational insights that I mentioned above. But they cannot be claimed by Christianity alone. Rather, Christianity is a *part* of the dynamics in the European synthesis of culture, which – given the distance to Troeltsch's time – now needs updating, because contrary movements have not stopped but in fact have become stronger in the twentieth and twenty-first century.[16] This further development is inherent to Troeltsch's method because it was he himself who emphasized that historical conceptions are embedded in contemporary assumptions of values and points of view. So the concept of

---

14   sen und seine Kultur auf die neuen Barbarenvölker übertrug und sie deren Bedürfnissen entsprechend abänderte. Das ist die ungeheure, welthistorische Bedeutung der christlichen Kirchen für unseren Kulturkreis" (Troeltsch, *Historismus*, 717 f.).

14   "Von diesen allgemeinen Kulturprinzipien 'lebt die europäische Welt ihr Leben.'" (Troeltsch, *Historismus*, 769).

15   Islam, whose significance for Europe Troeltsch does not explain in detail, does not for him belong to European cultural synthesis: "There is no joint synthesis of culture for both worlds," (Troeltsch, *Historismus*, 727: "Es gibt keine gemeinsame Kultursynthese für beide Welten").

16   Petra Bahr also pleads for a description of religious identity in Europe that includes agonal forces and contrary dynamics. See Petra Bahr, "Religion und Säkularität in Europa – ein gezähmter Widerspruch" in *Protestantismus und europäische Kultur*, ed. Petra Bahr et al. (Gütersloh: Gütersloher Verlagshaus, 2007), 94.

European cultural synthesis does not understand Europe in an essentialist way, but as a dynamic and dialectical movement that is open to new factors, influences and players. "Determining essence is designing essence", as Troeltsch once splendidly noted.[17]

Following this concept, we have to add two features to current European cultural synthesis that churches could collaborate with. Firstly, the memory of humanitarian catastrophes that totalitarian systems unleashed in the twentieth century despite the rational ethics of humanity and Christian ethics in Europe. This memory is an essential part of the European identity and at the same time part of the enlightened Christian consciousness. The deep anthropological insight of Christianity knows the dark side of the human person as still made in God's image and able to take responsibility for sin and guilt. Healing memories is an important concept that allows us to face past atrocities and guilt, and to find reconciliation through forgiveness and new solidarity between perpetrators and victims.

The second feature is to integrate Judaism and Islam into the cultural synthesis. In this context, the religions do not stand at the same level because there were Jewish contributions, but these were marginalized for long periods. We have to rediscover and to tell them in a new way. Islam has become visible in Europe through migration, and as a result of the influx of refugees and asylum-seekers. Now Muslims are to be recognized as an equal player in the European culture of religion.[18]

What could be the current task of churches in this matter? Instead of reclaiming a backward Christian Europe the task of the churches is to go on the offensive and to speak up for Europe as a sphere of religious freedom to prevent social divisions caused by different religious orientations. This insight is theologically well-founded because religious freedom is directly connected to the Protestant movement. So churches have to defend and broaden religious freedom within the limits of law and security. That includes defending oppressed minorities and helping to resolve religious conflicts. Churches in Germany did precisely that in the cases of the religious slaughtering of animals and circumcision in Germany a few years ago when courts of justice in Germany prohibited these rites. They supported finding legal regulations that allow Jews and Muslims to practise their rites.

---

[17]   Ernst Troeltsch, "Was heißt 'Wesen des Christentums'?" in id., *Zur religiösen Lage, Religionsphilosophie und Ethik* (Gesammelte Schriften II) (Tübingen: Mohr, 1922), 451: "Wesensbestimmung ist Wesensgestaltung."

[18]   This includes the recognition of contemporary Islamic concepts of Europe, see Vivien Neugebauer, *Europa im Islam – Islam in Europa. Islamische Konzepte zur Vereinbarkeit von religiöser und bürgerlicher Zugehörigkeit,* (Frankfurt am Main: Peter Lang Edition, 2016).

These days, the major challenge in this context is to deal with anti-Semitism and Islamophobia, both of which are increasing in European states. This, however, is a reaction to terrorist attacks in the few last years, to migrants and asylum-seekers who have left Africa or fled the hostilities in Syria and Iraq and entered EU-member states in great numbers. The reasons for anti-Semitism and Islamophobia are very complex, and I cannot focus on them here. But they are obstacles to establishing tolerance as a feature of the European culture of religion.

One important step could be to integrate these religions into the European cultural synthesis. Do we understand Islam as "the other", as Europe's opposite or enemy?[19] The US sociologist José Casanova speaks of "Europe's fear of religion,"[20] increased by the new visibility of Islam. If we understand demarcation from Islam as a feature of Christian Europe,[21] we will only achieve an attitude of "open and hospitable Europe" that "accepts"[22] Islamic migrants in a friendly way. But this will not be enough, because the task is to give migrants a feeling of belonging. And that is more than just hospitality. Churches could activate their concepts of tolerance, dialogue and cooperation to support this goal without neglecting their own tradition or their own understanding of faith and truth. The contrary movements in Europe include discussion, conflict and the struggle for truth – but in a peaceful way. The social divisions intensified by anti-Semitism and Islamophobia cannot be mitigated by the law alone. Rather, special efforts are necessary to break down hate, fear and prejudices. Dealing with this conflict is a task for *all* institutions of education. But religious communities in particular can set a good example by being open to dialogue and by understanding and supporting the feeling of belonging among Muslims in Europe. In this field, churches have to perform a pioneering role in society, something that might include risks. The Church of England and the regional churches in Germany have engaged themselves in this way during the last decades and are in this respect ahead of their time. Comparing this with the French situation, Grace Davie shows why the Established Church "are of particular importance in guaranteeing tolerance, in the sense of sustaining a [...] secure place for religious minorities".[23] I think this analysis includes the churches in Germany as well, and I hope for the future that

---

[19]   See Otto Kallscheuer, *Zur Zukunft des Abendlandes* (Springe: zu Klampen, 2009), 104.

[20]   See José Casanova, *Europas Angst vor dem Islam*, trans. Rolf Schieder (Berlin: Berlin University Press, 2009).

[21]   See Mariano Delgado, "Europa als christliches Projekt", in *Europa: Ein christliches Projekt? Beiträge zum Verhältnis von Religion und europäischer Identität*, ed. Urs Andermatt (Stuttgart: Kohlhammer, 2008), 47.

[22]   See Delgado, "Europa als christliches Projekt," 56.

[23]   Grace Davie, "European Identity, European Unity and the Christian Tradition", 107 below.

these contributions to establishing a liberal culture free of fear could be a model for other states and regions of the world.

By giving Muslims a feeling of belonging, it is important to sustain and develop the enlightened level of theological reflection of Christian faith. The academic origin of the Reformation and the academic training of clergy could serve as examples for other religions that are intended to gain a sense of belonging in European countries.[24] Against the background of increasing religious fundamentalism and increasing rational secularity, the significance of open-minded and self-reflective theology is of the utmost importance.

A specific aspect of the European "cultural synthesis" is the freedom not to be religious. It is an essential part of Europe that we have to acknowledge laical societies and the fact that many people are atheists and support secular ideologies. At this point, the churches should resist the temptation to establish a coalition of religious or interreligious forces to combat the so-called spirit of secularism or relativism of values. From a Protestant perspective, it should not be possible to fight against the modern world or profane reason. Against the background of Martin Luther's doctrine of God's two reigns, we have to respect people's freedom not to be religious, and to set reason and human law free in God's reign of the world, restricted by common values. So the further development of European religious culture also includes the opportunity of the negation of faith because it is not only part of the European history of religion, but is also embedded in the Protestant doctrine of the freedom of conscience.

IV. Mitigating the cost of social divisions caused by modern life

I rejected the concept of "hospitality" to describe the task of dealing with the European culture of religion. But "hospitality" would be much more appropriate to describe the task of dealing with social divisions connected with Europe and globalization.

We should mention three aspects.

Following the commandment to love one's neighbour, churches do a lot in their welfare and social institutions to help, support and give strength to poor people. In the political sphere, churches are social advocates for people who have no voice in public. Bishop Bedford-Strohm has impressively analysed and propa-

---

[24]   See Arnulf von Scheliha, "Religiöse Pluralität an der Universität. Chancen und Probleme staatlicher Steuerung und fachlicher Selbstbestimmung – am Beispiel der Etablierung des Faches Islamische Studien / Theologie an deutschen Universitäten", in id., *Religionspolitik. Beiträge zur politischen Ethik und zur politischen Dimension des religiösen Pluralismus* (Tübingen: Mohr Siebeck, 2018).

gated this "option for the poor".[25] I have nothing to add, except to give the hint that this social role of advocacy can only be played credibly if churches perform their institutional role as an employer in an exemplary way. If we claim credibility from other institutions such as the state or businesses, then we have to be credible ourselves – otherwise, we replicate social divisions.

More relevant to our theme is the next point of hospitality. As local, regional, national and European institutions, churches cultivate a network that can nurture a cosmopolitan consciousness that has effects at all levels. I follow Ben Ryan's description of the critical role of churches despite the difficulties it might have. Their "constant presence and commitment"[26] in local, regional, national and global dimensions predestine churches to realize social responsibility. That is a major difference to political responsibility, which feels responsible firstly to its duty of office and to its electors. Political responsibility tends to be restricted by given limits. Christian responsibility transcends given borders and focuses on problems in a multi-perspectival way. Hence, this universal dimension of Christian ethics includes consideration of problems and people beyond the border. Otherwise, we could not sort out global problems like climate change or the exploitation of natural resources, and plea for political solutions. Let me give an example. During the so-called refugee crisis, Christians dealt with a desperate situation beyond the European borders and made productive contributions to mitigating the distress of refugees and to offering incoming refugees hospitality. Many people are still helping refugees in Germany by welcoming them, teaching them German, or supporting them when they interact with administrative bodies and courts. Despite all the criticism levelled at the German government and churches, I think it was right to allow the refugees to come in 2015 by adopting the Old Testament tradition concerning strangers and refugees, to break down the pressure on EU-borders, and to help governments to deal with the wave of refugees. Naturally, churches also have to consider the needs of local members and people. But we don't play off the global dimension of Christian ethics against the needs of local or national responsibility, as some strict defenders of the Protestant doctrine of God's two reigns do.[27] Just the example of Europe shows that we can no longer think of this doctrine in terms of the nation state. Rather, we have to relate the distinction between God's two reigns to the European and international forms

---

[25]   See Heinrich Bedford-Strohm, *Vorrang für die Armen. Auf dem Weg zu einer theologischen Theorie der Gerechtigkeit* (Gütersloh: Kaiser/Gütersloher Verlagshaus, 1993); Heinrich Bedford-Strohm, "Öffentliche Theologie in der Zivilgesellschaft," in *Grundtexte Öffentliche Theologie,* ed. Florian Höhne and Frederike van Oorschoot (Leipzig: Evangelische Verlagsanstalt, 2015).

[26]   Ben Ryan, "A Nation Divided against Itself?", 77 above.

[27]   See Ulrich H.J. Körtner, "Gesinnungs- und Verantwortungsethik in der Flüchtlingspolitik," *Zeitschrift für Evangelische Ethik* 60 (2016).

of governance that we need to solve current ecological, social and political problems. Churches with their local bases, cross-border networks and universal ethics can help to establish and stabilize trans-border responsibility and to prevent withdrawal into national spheres.

This insight will be important after Brexit because new borders will be constructed and new social divisions will emerge. This scenario has no precedent. Brexit will probably establish new borders, new social divisions and a new economic situation. It is the task not only of politicians but also of civil society and churches to activate the means to help break through possible new political, social or mental borders. We should be prepared.

Experiences in European history could guide us in the future. Churches could mitigate the costs of social division as a consequence of modern life because their networks are present all over the world. So they could do both: strengthen the traditional sense of home by being present locally, and offer their hospitality to visiting or incoming people. Churches, as well as global networks such as scientific communities or NGOs, could make an important contribution to transcending borders and bridging social divisions.

V. A final Protestant remark

Churches have to remember that they do not represent Christianity as a whole. In our Lutheran tradition, we cultivate the distinction between visible and invisible church. That means: mitigating social divisions and developing Europe in a Christian sense do not depend on churches and their activities alone. Churches are important but not exclusive agencies of Christianity. As I have tried to show using Troeltsch's notion of "cultural synthesis", we have to distinguish between the plurality of Christian churches and confessional cultures on the one hand, and the normative foundations of politically organized Europe on the other, which can be identified and acknowledged in Christian perspective as related to the core of Biblical message. So, the foundations of Europe can be identified as a transformation of Christian insights into secular institutions that guarantee peace and freedom, especially freedom of religion.[28] Finally, Christianity is realized in the performance of individual responsibility by individual players in politics, the economy and society, who act to build peace and protect human rights. In the broader understanding, churches may trust to the power and effectiveness of God's Word and Holy Spirit both *in* churches and *extra muros ecclesiarum* in the ongoing European project.

---

[28]   See Arnulf von Scheliha, "Religiöser Pluralismus und Theorie des Christentums," in id., *Religionspolitik. Beiträge zur politischen Ethik und zur politischen Dimension des religiösen Pluralismus* (Tübingen: Mohr Siebeck, 2018).

Bibliography

AfD. "Grundsatzprogramm." Accessed February 20, 2019. https://www.afd.de/grund satzprogramm/.

AfD. "DEXIT – The Exit as Last Option." Accessed February 20, 2019. https://www.afd.de/wp-content/uploads/sites/111/2019/02/AfD_Europawahlprogramm_A5-hoch_web.pdf.

Bahr, Petra. "Religion und Säkularität in Europa – ein gezähmter Widerspruch." In *Protestantismus und europäische Kultur*, edited by Petra Bahr, Aleida Assmann, Wolfgang Huber, and Bernhard Schlink, 85–96. Gütersloh: Gütersloher Verlagshaus, 2007.

Bedford-Strohm, Heinrich. *Vorrang für die Armen. Auf dem Weg zu einer theologischen Theorie der Gerechtigkeit.* Gütersloh: Kaiser/Gütersloher Verlagshaus, 1993.

Bedford-Strohm, Heinrich. "Öffentliche Theologie in der Zivilgesellschaft." In *Grundtexte Öffentliche Theologie*, edited by Florian Höhne and Frederike van Oorschoot, 211–226. Leipzig: Evangelische Verlagsanstalt, 2015.

Casanova, José. *Europas Angst vor dem Islam.* Translated by Rolf Schieder. Berlin: Berlin University Press, 2009.

Delgado, Mariano. "Europa als christliches Projekt." In *Europa: Ein christliches Projekt? Beiträge zum Verhältnis von Religion und europäischer Identität*, edited by Urs Andermatt, 35–58. Stuttgart: Kohlhammer, 2008.

EKD. *Evangelische Kirche und freiheitliche Demokratie. Der Staat des Grundgesetzes als Angebot und Aufgabe. Eine Denkschrift der Evangelischen Kirche in Deutschland.* Gütersloh: Gütersloher Verlagshaus, 1985.

EKD. "Statement by the Council of the Evangelical Church in Germany (EKD) on the situation of Europe, Brussels, 23 April 2016." Accessed February 20, 2019. https://www.ekd.de/ekd_en/ds_doc/20160423_erklaerung_zur_lage_europas_en.pdf.

EKD. "We continue to pin our hopes on Europe." Accessed February 20, 2019. https://www.ekd.de/ekd_en/ds_doc/ecumenical_statement_of_signing_of_rome_treaties.pdf.

Heinig, Hans Michael Heinig, ed. *Aneignung des Gegebenen. Entstehung und Wirkung der Demokratie-Denkschrift der EKD.* Tübingen: Mohr Siebeck, 2017.

Kallscheuer, Otto. *Zur Zukunft des Abendlandes.* Springe: zu Klampen, 2009.

Körtner, Ulrich H.J. "Gesinnungs- und Verantwortungsethik in der Flüchtlingspolitik." *Zeitschrift für Evangelische Ethik* 60 (2016): 282–296.

Lepp, Claudia and Kurt Nowak, ed. *Evangelische Kirche im geteilten Deutschland (1945–1989/90).* Göttingen: Vandenhoeck & Ruprecht, 2001.

Neugebauer, Vivien. *Europa im Islam – Islam in Europa. Islamische Konzepte zur Vereinbarkeit von religiöser und bürgerlicher Zugehörigkeit.* Frankfurt am Main: Peter Lang Edition, 2016.

Rat der Evangelische Kirche in Deutschland and Katholische Kirche Deutsche Bischofskonferenz. *Demokratie braucht Tugenden. Gemeinsames Wort des Rates der Evangelischen Kirche in Deutschland und der Deutschen Bischofskonferenz zur Zukunft unseres demokratischen Gemeinwesens.* Hannover: Kirchenamt der Evangelischen Kirche in Deutschland and Bonn: Sekretariat der Deutschen Bischofskonferenz, 2006.

Scheliha, Arnulf von. *Protestantische Ethik des Politischen.* Tübingen: Mohr Siebeck, 2013.

Scheliha, Arnulf von. "Politik im neutralen, säkularen Staat – Wie reagier(t)en die Religionen?" *Bibel und Liturgie ... in kulturellen Räumen* 90 (2017): 181–188.

Scheliha, Arnulf von. "Religiöser Pluralismus und Theorie des Christentums." In id., *Religionspolitik. Beiträge zur politischen Ethik und zur politischen Dimension des religiösen Pluralismus*, 210–224. Tübingen: Mohr Siebeck, 2018.

Scheliha, Arnulf von. "Religiöse Pluralität an der Universität. Chancen und Probleme staatlicher Steuerung und fachlicher Selbstbestimmung – am Beispiel der Etablierung des Faches Islamische Studien / Theologie an deutschen Universitäten." In id., *Religionspolitik. Beiträge zur politischen Ethik und zur politischen Dimension des religiösen Pluralismus*, 227–239. Tübingen: Mohr Siebeck, 2018.

Troeltsch, Ernst. *Der Historismus und seine Probleme* (Gesammelte Schriften III). Tübingen: Mohr, 1922.

Troeltsch, Ernst. "Was heißt 'Wesen des Christentums'?" In id., *Zur religiösen Lage, Religionsphilosophie und Ethik* (Gesammelte Schriften II), 368–451. Tübingen: Mohr, 1922.

6. European Identity, European Unity and the Christian Tradition

Grace Davie

Introduction

At the conference from which this paper originated, I was asked to address the following question: "To what extent does the identity and therefore the unity of Europe continue to depend on a common Christian heritage?" I responded in two rather different ways. Thus the first section of the paper will look at the Christian tradition in all its diversity as a formative factor in the making and re-making of Europe, mindful that there are two further strands in this history: Greek rationalism and Roman organization. What is their relative impact in the present situation and how is this likely to develop? The second section turns to the institutional forms that "carry" the Christian tradition, paying particular attention to the historically dominant churches of different confessions that are present in every European society. The Church of England forms one case study among others, in which I will underline the advantages of a "weak" established church as a place of welcome and dialogue in society as a whole.

Both sections should be read against the current situation with respect to religion in Europe, which can be summarized as follows.

Five factors must be taken into account if we are to understand this situation fully. These are:

1. the role of the historic churches in shaping European culture.
2. an awareness that these churches still have a place at particular moments in the lives of European people, though they are no longer able to influence – let alone discipline – the beliefs and behaviour of the great majority of the population; nor should they in a modern democracy.
3. an observable change in the actively religious constituencies of the continent, which operate increasingly on a model of choice, rather than a model of obligation or duty.
4. the arrival into Europe of groups of people from many different parts of the world, and with very different religious aspirations from those seen in the host society.

5.   the reactions of Europe's more secular constituencies to the growing presence
     of religion in public as well as private life.

Each of the above factors merits careful consideration in its own right. One way of
drawing them together, however, is to recall the two rather different things that
are happening at once in twenty-first century Europe. On the one hand are the
growing levels of secularity, or simply indifference, which lead in turn to an
inevitable decline in religious knowledge as well as in religious belief. On the
other is a series of increasingly urgent debates about the place of religion in public
and private life, prompted by the need to accommodate new populations who
bring with them very different ways of being religious. In short Europeans talk
more about something that they do less. This largely unexpected combination is
difficult to manage – unsurprisingly given the clashes of interest embedded in
these encounters.

The Christian tradition in the formation of Europe

O'Connell, amongst others, identifies three elements that come together in the
unity that we call Europe: these are Judaeo-Christian monotheism, Greek rationalism and Roman organization.[1] These formative influences shift and adapt over
time, but their combinations can be seen forming and re-forming a way of life that
we have come to recognize as European. In what follows the emphasis will lie on
two of these influences in particular: the Christian tradition and Greek (secular)
rationalism.[2]

Regarding the former, one illustration will suffice: the Christian tradition has
had an irreversible effect in determining the most basic categories of human existence (time and space) in this part of the world. Both week and year follow the
Christian cycle, even if the major festivals of the Christian calendar are beginning
to lose their resonance for large sections of the population. Many of them are
nonetheless retained as a framework for public holidays. Sunday, moreover,
remains distinctive despite the fact that the notion of a "day of rest" has largely
been discarded.

The same is true of space. Wherever you look in Europe, Christian churches
predominate, some of which retain huge symbolic value for the populations that
surround them. And from the largest city to the smallest village, European people
orient themselves with reference to religious buildings even if they seldom enter

---

1   James O'Connell, *The Making of Modern Europe: Strengths, Constraints and Resolutions*
    (Bradford: University of Bradford, 1991).

2   In a short paper I will use the term Christian, rather than Judaeo-Christian. I am aware
    however of the sensitivities of these terms.

them for worship. The whole of Europe, moreover, is divided into parishes – a territorial model with civic as well as religious connotations. For centuries, the parish determined the parameters of life for the great majority of European people from the cradle to the grave. Its significance has weakened over time, but the residues still resonate, sometimes in unexpected ways. This is not to deny that in some parts of the continent (notably the larger cities) the situation is changing, and changing fast. The skyline, in itself, is indicative of growing religious diversity.

Such diversity has been brought about by in-migration. The initial influx was linked to an urgent need for labour in the mid post-war decades as West European economies (notably the UK, France, West Germany and the Netherlands) expanded rapidly. An entirely different constituency found its way to West Europe at a later stage. The 2004 (or in some cases 2007) enlargements of the European Union permitted the easy movement of people from one part of Europe to another. The significant number of Poles now living in Britain is but one example of this shift. Open borders, however, have become increasingly contentious as the number of migrants has risen, swelled in recent years by those fleeing from violence in the Middle East or from extreme poverty in parts of Africa.

Equally important in this respect is the shift in focus regarding the debate about migration. In the mid post-war decades, the emphasis was largely on ethnicity, but from the 1990s on, there has been a much greater awareness of religion. In Britain, the publication of Salman Rushdie's *Satanic Verses* marked a turning point.[3] It was the moment when Muslims from many different nationalities and backgrounds found a common voice.[4] Significantly this coincided with the decade in which the geo-political order began to re-align, revealing renewed and at times violent expressions of religion in many parts of the globe.

A second, rather different shift can be found in the growing numbers of "nones"; that is the sector – or more accurately sectors – of European society that declare that they have no religious affiliation. The data indicate that this constituency varies considerably across Europe and is especially prevalent among young adults. Bullivant offers an excellent overview.[5] The "nones", moreover, are a heterogeneous group. As Woodhead (a close observer of the British case) puts

---

[3]   Salman Rushdie, *The Satanic Verses* (London; New York: Viking-Penguin, 1988).

[4]   See Paul Weller, *A Mirror for our Times: "The Rushdie Affair" and the Future of Multiculturalism* (London: Continuum, 2009).

[5]   Stephen Bullivant, *Europe's Young Adults and Religion. Findings from the European Social Survey (2014–16)* (St Mary's University, Twickenham, London: Benedict XVI Centre for Religion and Society, 2018).

this: only a minority are convinced atheists; the maybes, doubters and don't knows are just as present, "plus 5.5 per cent who definitely believe in God".[6]

More provocative are the sharply secular voices of the "new atheists" articulating not indifference, but hostility to religion. For this constituency, religion should not simply be tolerated but should be countered, criticized and exposed by rational argument. Religion in other words is toxic; this is not a question of live and let live but of active campaigning to expose both the falsity of religious argument and the damage that ensues. Taken together these tendencies – a drift from the churches on the one hand and a radical critique of religion on the other – indicate a rebalancing in the formative influences outlined above: secular constituencies of whatever kind are growing in confidence at the expense of the historic churches, a trend that is unlikely to reverse.

All that said, the middle ground – in the form of nominal Christianity – remains dominant, though more so in some parts of Europe than others (see below). A recent survey emphasizes this fact. Entitled "Being Christian in Western Europe" (Pew Research Centre 2018), it starts by affirming what we know already: that "most Western Europeans continue to identify as Christians, though few regularly attend church".[7] The core of the report goes further, however, pursuing a particular theme arising from this finding: the fact that the religious, political and cultural views of non-practising Christians differ both from those of church-attending Christians and from those of religiously unaffiliated adults. The variations are followed through in terms of attitudes towards churches and religious organizations on the one hand and immigrants and religious minorities on the other. A much-quoted headline is the following:

> Christian identity in Western Europe is associated with higher levels of negative sentiment toward immigrants and religious minorities. On balance, self-identified Christians – whether they attend church or not – are more likely than religiously unaffiliated people to express negative views of immigrants, as well as of Muslims and Jews.[8]

In this context, moreover, self-identification as "Christian" is as likely to mean "not Muslim" as it is to mean "not secular". Circumstances alter cases.

One further observation is important. The factors outlined above are differently weighted depending on (a) the part of Europe under review and (b) the particular histories of individual countries. The latter crosscut the former. For

---

6   Linda Woodhead, "The Rise of 'No Religion' in Britain: The Emergence of a New Cultural Majority," *Journal of the British Academy* 4 (2016): 250.

7   Pew Research Centre, *Being Christian in Western Europe*, 2018 (May): 6, accessed February 27, 2019 http://www.pewforum.org/2018/05/29/being-christian-in-western-europe/.

8   Ibid. 9.

example: the Orthodox churches of Eastern Europe, and the cultures that they represent, are for the most part growing in confidence, very often at the expense of religious minorities, both Christian and other. The Bulgarian Church, however, is noticeably weaker than its neighbours in terms of finance as well as personnel. Rather similar variations can be found in Catholic Europe where (in the west) the Italian and Portuguese churches remain strong in contrast to those in France or Belgium which struggle to make an impact. In Spain, the shift from the former to the latter situation has happened in a generation. In Northern Europe, the process of secularization is more advanced than it is further south but takes different forms in different places: Lutheran churches, supported by church tax or its modern equivalent, sustain relatively high levels of membership but much lower levels of practice or belief. The Church of England – never as dominant as its continental equivalents – is eroded on both fronts and is rapidly becoming one minority among others in a society where "no religion" attracts around 50 % of the population.

In short, the Christian tradition remains a framing factor in the making and re-making of Europe and will continue to do so, though more strongly in some parts of the continent than in others. Particularly in the north and west of Europe, this is increasingly challenged by secular currents (and the constituencies that carry them) in both their assertive and less assertive forms. Both the Christian tradition and its secular alter egos are obliged, moreover, to take account of the growing diversity of Europe's religions. It is equally clear that both can be generous and accommodating in their responses, but this cannot simply be assumed. Indifference, bordering on hostility, can take secular as well as religious forms.

States and state churches

A broad-brush profile of religion in Europe provides the background for a more detailed discussion of church and state relationships; these in turn constitute the parameters within which religious life on a national level takes place. It is helpful to set this discussion within the following framework, taken from David Martin's seminal work on secularization in the Western world, *A General Theory of Secularization.*[9] Following Martin, Europe is a unity by virtue of having possessed one Caesar and one God (hence the commonalities of faith and culture set out above); it is a diversity by the existence of nations. The patterns of European religion derive from the tensions and partnerships between religion and the search for national integrity and identity.[10] These tensions and partnerships are enduring processes which have dominated four centuries of European history. Should

---

[9]   David, Martin, *A General Theory of Secularization* (Oxford: Blackwell, 1978).
[10]   Ibid.

we be surprised, therefore, that they continue to resonate in the debates surrounding the nature and identity of both Europe and the European Union as this unfolds in the twenty-first century? Brexit, and its aftermath, is but one stage in a longer journey.

Two further preliminaries are important. The first is to emphasize once again the territorial nature of Europe's historic churches, a factor that operates at national (state church), regional (diocese), as well as the local or parish level already mentioned. The significance of these churches in forming national identities follows from this. The second is to appreciate that in certain parts of the continent, the historic connections between church and state were comprehensively ruptured in the second half of the twentieth century. Specifically, in those countries which were part of the Soviet bloc, former state churches became in many places part – a very effective part – of the opposition to communism in both its structural and ideological forms. The Polish case is well-known. Rather different is the East German example where a tiny, compromised and infiltrated Lutheran Church became the meeting place for resistance at the crucial moment. In 1989, nonviolent demonstrators assembling in the Nikolaikirche in Leipzig became more and more numerous, spreading out into the surrounding streets and chanting *"Wir sind das Volk"* (*"We are the people"*). Surprised at the size of the protest, the security forces backed off.

In what follows, the focus will lie on the Church of England as an example of what might be achieved by a "weak" established church in the current situation, meaning by this a numerically eroded church with a distinctive history – one of partial rather than total monopoly in a country that has housed significant religious minorities for centuries rather than decades. In order to appreciate such benefits, it is worth reflecting on the disquieting situations further East in, say, Poland or Hungary where the historic churches – or to be more precise, elements within these – have become the focus for sentiments that are sharply hostile both to immigration as such and to the new forms of religion that migrants bring with them. All too often such hostility is bolstered by an uncritical elision between national identity and the national church. In 2016, the contrast between Hungarian reactions to the migrants traversing Europe and the generous inclusion encouraged by the present Pope was striking. For Pope Francis, the injunction to welcome the stranger is seen as a gospel imperative; for Viktor Orban and his supporters, welcoming the migrant is deemed contrary to the national interest.

Such reactions are disturbing. They should be seen however in an historical context. As David Martin has taught us, the complex relationships between church and state do not simply fall from the sky.[11] They are the consequence of detailed histories that place recent events within a larger narrative in which the dominant church is seen as a bulwark against foreign invasion. The role of the

---

[11]   Ibid.

Catholic Church in Polish resistance to communism has already been mentioned. In Hungary, the details are different but a century and a half of Ottoman rule (1541–1699) continues to resonate.

The Church of England: a "weak" established church

It is well-known that a disproportionate number of Anglicans voted "leave" in the 2016 referendum.[12] The meticulous analysis that underpins this assertion sifts a wide variety of data and comes to the following conclusion: "In short, identifying as 'Church of England' is a major independent predictor of voting Brexit. The effect remains even when other factors are controlled for".[13] Regular religious attendance reduces the tendency to vote "leave" but does not eliminate this entirely.

Why did this happen? Why in other words did Anglicans vote to "leave" rather than to "remain"? The main incentive, it emerges, was hostility to the European Union, seeing this as "an overly bureaucratic and 'interfering' body without sufficient democratic accountability".[14] Additional reasons are pride in English identity, recognizing the place of the Church of England in this, and a corresponding wish to protect this identity from external "threat", very often perceived as a consequence of migration. In voting "leave" in disproportionate numbers, moreover, Anglican people were resisting the advice of their Bishops – a nice outworking of an old adage: that those in the chancel read *The Guardian* whilst those in the pew prefer *The Telegraph*.

In their conclusion, Smith and Woodhead invite caution in the use of the term "populism" regarding the place of "religion" in this outcome. Specifically, it would be unwise to use the same term for the role that religion (more especially Anglicanism) played in the Brexit vote in the UK with the role that evangelicals played in the election of Donald Trump in the US later in the same year (2016). These are rather different phenomena.

In the remainder of this section I will consider the place of the Church of England in post-Brexit Britain from a different perspective. This needs to be set in context. The following table uses data from the British Social Attitudes surveys from 1983–2011 to reveal a decisive shift in British society. Self-affiliating Anglicans, both nominal and practising, are diminishing fast as a proportion of the population at the expense of the "nones" – a change that is more marked in Britain than it is in most parts of Europe (see above).

---

[12]   See Greg Smith and Linda Woodhead, "Religion and Brexit: Populism and the Church of England," *Religion, State and Society*, 46 (2018).

[13]   Ibid., 208.

[14]   Ibid., 315.

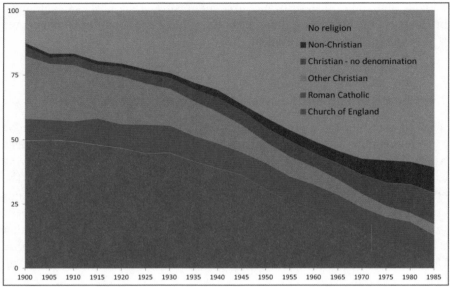

Source: British Social Attitudes surveys 1983–2011, pooled. Chart created by Siobhan McAndrew, British Religion in Numbers (http://www.brin.ac.uk/figures/). Creative Commons Attribution-Share Alike 2.0 England and Wales (CC BY-SA 2.0 UK).

Figure 1: Religious affiliation in Great Britain by year of birth (five year cohorts)

What then is the position of the Church of England in this new – and continually changing – context? I will respond by highlighting some often over-looked advantages. Specifically, a numerically diminished state (or established) Church has opportunities for action and initiative denied to more dominant equivalents. Discerning its strengths from a distinctive and relatively pluralist past, it can use these imaginatively to welcome rather than exclude, and to encourage rather than to condemn. Such an approach counters the following oft-repeated assertion: that the present system (i. e. establishment) is no longer tenable in a society which is – at one and the same time – both more secular and more religiously diverse.

Put differently, I am of the opinion that the maintenance of a tolerant and pluralist society is enhanced by an established church. As an institution it is uniquely placed to promote and to sustain a constructive conversation about faith (of all kinds) at the centre rather than the margins of British (more properly English) society, an ever more necessary task. And quite apart from the merits of this situation, the aftermath of the Brexit referendum might be taken as a cautionary tale. It is one thing to decide by a narrow majority to leave the European Union; it is quite another to find a way forward that is acceptable to all parties. Might the same things happen in the case of disestablishment?

A French excursus

A comparison with the French case constitutes a post-script to this section, which unpacks a further paradox: France is both constitutionally and institutionally more democratic than Britain, but Britain is – or has been – more tolerant than France. Why is this so? The answer lies at least in part in a very different history of church-state connections in each society.

In Britain – as in most of Northern Europe – the historic churches were de-clericalized from the inside at the time of the Reformation. As a result, there was little tension between the various forms of Protestantism that emerged in the constituent countries of Britain and the secular state. There were, nonetheless, marked interdenominational conflicts, some of which had political consequences – most obviously at the time of the civil war in the seventeenth century. In France conversely, a hegemonic Catholic Church permitted little or no dissent from within, with the effect that the secularization process, when it could no longer be resisted, was markedly more conflictual. An intransigent Catholic Church clashed with an equally uncompromising secular state, underpinned by its own ideology: *laïcité*. An indication of just how different the two countries are is easily illustrated in the difficulties that British people have in grasping the meaning of this term. The reason, however, is clear: the British cannot understand the idea of *laïcité* because there is nothing in British society that can realistically be described as *laïque*.

Precisely this lacuna is central to the question under review. France (in terms of its Republican ideals, its elected second chamber and its developed *laïcité*) is more democratic than its neighbour across the Channel. Britain in contrast has retained its monarchy, its unelected second chamber and its established church. Paradoxically, however, Britain is – or has been until very recently – noticeably more tolerant than France. It is, moreover, the apparently "undemocratic" institutions just listed that are of particular importance in guaranteeing tolerance, in the sense of sustaining a relatively secure place for religious minorities in British society.

It is not possible in a short paper to work through the detail of each of these institutions. Particularly striking, however, is the following extract from a speech given by the Queen herself in 2012 at a multi-faith reception at Lambeth Palace, which speaks very directly to the underlying question. With reference to the Church of England, she says:

> Its role is not to defend Anglicanism to the exclusion of other religions. Instead, the Church has a duty to protect the free practice of all faiths in this country.

It certainly provides an identity and spiritual dimension for its own many adherents. But also, gently and assuredly, the Church of England has created an environment for other faith communities and indeed people of no faith to live freely. Woven into the fabric of this country, the Church has helped to build a better society – more and more in active co-operation for the common good with those of other faiths.[15]

How long this delicate arrangement will last is difficult to say. One point, however, is abundantly clear. In the continuing debates about establishment in this country, it is not usually the other-faith communities that encourage the separation of church and state. It is rather a growing, and increasingly vocal, secular lobby which argues for the exclusion of faith and faith communities of all kinds from public life.

Neither the French, nor the British situation is immutable. In France, President Macron is reaching out to the faith communities in new and unexpected ways. In April 2018, for example, the President accepted an invitation to an event organized by the French Bishops' Conference (CEF) at the Collège des Bernardins in Paris. The context for this meeting was the growing concerns of the French bishops regarding a wide range of issues: bioethics, immigration and the growing religious tensions all too evident in France. This – it is important to note – was the first time a French head of state had accepted an invitation by Catholic clergy to address such a meeting, in a country defined by its firm separation of church and state.

A perceptive commentary on this event can be found in *Le Monde*. It was written by a distinguished sociologist of religion and former President of the Ecole des Hautes Etudes en Sciences Sociales.[16] Danièle Hervieu-Léger starts by noting that simply the presence of the President in such a meeting sparked very different reactions: on the one hand were those shocked by the violation of *laïcité*; on the other were those hoping for renewed and close collaboration between church and state. A more constructive solution lies somewhere between the two: a way forward in which the French Catholic Church finds its rightful place in an increasingly pluralist society. No longer hegemonic, it still has much to give: in its theological questions (rather than answers) as much as in its support for the vulnerable. Faith demands action and cannot be totally privatized.

---

[15]   For the full text of the speech, see the official website of the Royal Family, accessed February 27, 2019, https://www.royal.uk/queens-speech-lambeth-palace-15-february-2012.

[16]   Danièle Hervieu-Léger, "Emmanuel Macron aux évêques: 'Un discours hors norme,'" *Le Monde*, April 11, 2018, https://www.lemonde.fr/idees/article/2018/04/11/emmanuel-macron-aux-eveques-un-discours-hors-norme_5283783_3232.html (accessed February 27, 2019).

In conclusion

An important element in President Macron's address was his recognition – once again controversial – of the role played by the Catholic Church in the long-term construction of French identity. Extrapolating from the French case to Europe as a whole, we can return thus to the question that I was asked to address in this paper: "To what extent does the identity and therefore the unity of Europe continue to depend on a common Christian heritage?"

I have argued that the Christian tradition in its diverse forms was and remains a formative factor in the building and rebuilding of Europe. It must however be balanced by an equally formative secular voice. And in the twenty-first century, both the Christian tradition and its secular counterpart have to operate within an increasingly diverse continent. How this will happen will vary considerably from place to place.

Key players in this process are the historic churches found in all European societies. Some remain dominant and some less so. All of them, however, are obliged to adjust to a continually changing situation. Out of very different histories, the Church of England and its French counterpart are finding new ways forward. The Church of England is deploying its established status in innovative ways not only to sustain the identity of its members, but also to permit a constructive conversation about faith (of all kinds) at the centre of English society. The French Catholic Church is emerging from a markedly more conflictual past to find its place in late modern French society, invited to do this – paradoxically – by the President of the Republic himself.

Bibliography

Bullivant, Stephen. *Europe's Young Adults and Religion. Findings from the European Social Survey (2014–16) to inform the 2018 Synod of Bishops.* St Mary's University, Twickenham, London: Benedict XVI Centre for Religion and Society, 2018.

Hervieu-Léger, Danièle. "Emmanuel Macron aux évêques: 'Un discours hors norme.'" *Le Monde*, April 11, 2018. https://www.lemonde.fr/idees/article/2018/04/11/emmanuel-macron-aux-eveques-un-discours-hors-norme_5283783_3232.html (accessed February 27, 2019).

Martin, David. *A General Theory of Secularization.* Oxford: Blackwell, 1978.

O'Connell, James. *The Making of Modern Europe: Strengths, Constraints and Resolutions,* University of Bradford Peace Research Reports. No. 26. Bradford: University of Bradford, 1991.

Pew Research Centre. *Being Christian in Western Europe,* 2018 (May). Accessed February 27, 2019. http://www.pewforum.org/2018/05/29/being-christian-in-western-europe/.

Rushdie, Salman. *The Satanic Verses.* London; New York: Viking-Penguin, 1988.

Smith, Greg and Woodhead, Linda. "Religion and Brexit: Populism and the Church of England." *Religion, State and Society,* 46 (2018): 206–25.

Weller, Paul. *A Mirror for our Times: "The Rushdie Affair" and the Future of Multiculturalism.* London: Continuum, 2009.

Woodhead, Linda. "The Rise of 'No Religion' in Britain: The Emergence of a New Cultural Majority." *Journal of the British Academy,* 4 (2016): 245–61.

III Response: What Can the European Churches Do?

7. Riches and Risks of Tackling Contemporary European Issues Ecumenically

Sarah Rowland Jones

I give you a new commandment, that you love one another. Just as I have loved you, you also should love one another. By this everyone will know that you are my disciples, if you have love for one another. John 13:34–35[1]

On the Sunday morning after the Brexit vote, I found myself in the BBC Radio Wales studio for a live broadcast about the referendum in the religious affairs programme *All Things Considered.* I was there broadly to defend the position of the Church in Wales' Bishops, who, like other Welsh church leaders, had called for a remain vote. And yet Wales had voted to leave by 52.5 % to 47.5 %, an only slightly smaller margin than England. Another panellist was the Vicar of Ebbw Vale, who heartily endorsed the 62 % leave vote of that area, the highest in Wales.

How and why did the Welsh Bishops fail? At first glance, a strong case can be made justifying their belief that such scriptural imperatives as pursing "good news for the poor" and "love your neighbour [of whatever nationality] as yourself" would be best served by a remain vote. But they, and other Welsh Christian leaders, failed to enunciate this in ways that those for whose good they desired to speak recognized themselves and their interests represented in public discourse. The Bishops were not found relevant or pertinent among many clergy and faithful, let alone among the wider public. More than that, their theological reasoning was found inadequate and unconvincing by considerable numbers within their own churches.

This is one snap-shot from a small corner of north-west Europe. Yet it illustrates some of the challenges of developing, and expressing, more subtle and profound theological responses to current socio-economic and political questions and trends we are facing within the EU, including within many member states, and more widely across Europe. Taking it as read that, as Rowan Williams is wont to

---

[1] All biblical quotations are taken from the New Revised Standard Version, Anglicized edition.

say, it takes the whole church to know the whole truth,[2] in this chapter I shall explore both the riches and the risks of tackling contemporary European issues ecumenically. While much applies to matters within the EU (of which Brexit is just one) my canvas covers the whole continent, and indeed touches on our place in the wider world. Here, in our geography, politics, economics, culture, faith and more besides, we have huge diversity, including both within and between our churches, so the task of reflecting deeply, speaking and acting together is daunting. But, by God's grace, we will do better by engaging with one another as we engage with the situations and trends that confront us than by each facing our own contexts separately.

Our starting point lies in committing ourselves to a praxis of thinking and acting Christianly. While we need to engage with the socio-economic and political culture around us in ways that effectively communicate, our approach must first be shaped by the central tenets of our own beliefs. Foremost, ours is an incarnational faith: we do not begin with abstract religious principles, philosophical axioms or political assumptions. We believe that God meets us, supremely in Jesus Christ who shared human life and death unqualifiedly, and through the Holy Spirit. Incarnate, redemptive, sacrificial love, triumphing over the destructiveness of sin and death, reaches into every circumstance of existence, as God engages with God's world: its individuals, its communities, its nations, and the entirety of creation. We are creatures of particular times and places: our histories shape us and our contexts compel us, and it is in our here-and-nows that our theological reflection comes out of our encounter with, and response to, the Living God.

Thus I shall emphasize incarnation and relationality as the basis of our ecumenical engagement, before turning to the lenses of sin and redemptive hope, as offering particular perspectives and insights on how we live out our shared life in Christ, for the sake of the world.

Incarnation and relationality

Beginning with incarnation and relationality grounds us in the here and now – a rubber-hits-the-road approach that calls for an intentionality both in the way we conduct our relationships with each other as Christian traditions in Europe, and in how we work together to "discern the signs of the times" (Matt 16:3). It is a call to bring the perspectives of God's redeeming love into the particularities of the broken and hurting contexts we now face. We always, and only, encounter God,

---

2   "Archbishop of Canterbury – 'Challenge and Hope' for the Anglican Communion," last modified June 27, 2006. https://www.anglicannews.org/news/2006/06/archbishop-of-canterbury-challenge-and-hope-for-the-anglican-communion.aspx.

and one another within the body of Christ, in the specificity of our time and place, and so we can dare to believe we are called to weave a richer, more textured, tapestry that can address the complexities of the socio-economic and political challenges before us.

This is not to set aside the more traditional grounding, content and conduct of our ecumenical engagement, but to graft their achievements and riches into a deeper, broader abiding in Christ. Among the shifting of focus and fresh dynamics this can bring, importantly, it can help safeguard us from temptations to theologize in ways that become "explorations of truths about God", and from superficial applications of abstract "Christian principles". Instead, it roots us more deeply in continuing, dependent, engagement with God and explorations of the truths we find in him, for our world, in our time. It also keeps drawing us back to humble consciousness of our own inescapable proclivities to perennial forms of temptation and sin, which inevitably find expression in whatever structures and practices we embrace, within our Christian relationships as well as within our world. Yet, gloriously, the more we are enabled to relate to one another in the unfolding shared relationship of our ongoing relationship within the body of Christ, honest about all our fallibilities, the more we shall know the grace of his redeeming love powerfully at work among us.

Let me focus first on this conscious turn from the world's tendency, in the discourse of public life, to view ourselves as autonomous subjects, holding Cartesian views of truth as reducible to cognitive propositions of single unambiguous meaning. Instead, we site ourselves on our knees, in humble, prayerful, receptive, engagement with the one who is "the Way, the Truth, the Life." Our relationship with Jesus Christ constitutes the basis for our relationship with one another, through which we pursue together the life-giving way of truth as found in him for our continent at this time.

As demonstrated though the Global Christian Forum[3], developing mutual trust and respect through recognizing one another "in Christ", alongside traditional forms of ecumenical engagement, strengthens and broadens the capacity of Christians of different traditions to journey together. Through dialogue that begins with sharing testimony to our relationship with Christ, we hear one another speak as children of the same heavenly Father. Our lives declare that he is our "Abba", and, even if we use very different human language, we discover ourselves recognizing God's Spirit bearing witness with one another's spirits that we are each children of God, and heirs, co-heirs with Christ (cf. Rom 8:16-17).

Thus, knowing that Christ is not divided (1 Cor 1:13) means that to recognize relationship with Christ in one another is, by implication, to recognize indestructible, imperishable, eternally abiding relationship between ourselves, no matter

---

[3] See the official website of the Global Christian Forum, http://www.globalchristianforum. org/.

how easy or difficult we find it to agree on matters couched in the language of faith and order. To belong to Christ means to belong to one another. This is a given – a gift that lies not in our own hands, but in the hands of the one who bestows the gift of faith. We can no longer objectify one another on the basis of otherness. There is a world of difference between asking "If this is what they believe, how can they possibly be real Christians?" and asking "Since you are my brother, my sister, in Christ, can you explain how you adopt this formulation of faith, this practice, this way of Christian living?"

Not only does such an approach have the capacity to breathe new life into longstanding relationships. It also confronts us with a spiritual imperative that cannot be ducked to work ever more closely together, on the widest possible basis. Even where the Lund principle of 1952 – that we should in all things act together except where deep differences of conviction compel us to act separately – offers us ways out, we are continually recalled to return to the charge, and wrestle together again. For division within the body of Christ can never be an acceptable resting point.

This particular way of placing Christ at the centre of our relationships with one another has also extended engagement with Christian traditions whose self-understanding is not primarily rooted in faith and order concepts, including Charismatic, Pentecostal, African Instituted and other "new" church movements. That said, the currency of "testimony" can still be uncomfortable for many – and there is a risk that after initial encounter, it is hard to know where to take the substance of our engagement next if we look only to traditional practices of ecumenism. But this may be to frame the question wrongly, whereas deepening spiritual encounter, including facing the issues of the world together "on our knees" and not only through our minds, is part of what we need to learn to do better. It is also the means of finding continuing fuel, through the empowering of the Spirit, as we persist in the unrelentingly difficult task of preaching God's word into our increasingly secularising world, which so often deliberately chooses deafness in response.

Recognizing our shared identity and existence in Christ should ground us in boundless common hope – even when at first glance it seems we face the daunting prospect of finding one another as mutually incomprehensible as seeing is to the ear, or hearing to the nose (1 Cor 12:17). There may well be hard wrestling to be done around matters on which we diverge, whether as Christians or across the conflicts of our political contexts. But we are called boldly to grapple in honesty and truthfulness, safe in the wider context of knowing we are held together by and in God's love. It is a challenge to show and share this radical love, across any and all possible gulfs. But our capacity to demonstrate reconciliation and model living well with difference and mutual respect, and thus our ability to be Christ's reconcilers, is one of our most urgent callings in a world where polarization and division have increasing traction.

The sin that divides

It is easy enough to look at the world around us, and diagnose it as fallen, broken and sinful, in need of divine redemption in all areas. More challenging to us – to our self-image and latent pride, rather more than to our intellectual capacities, I suspect – is to recognize ourselves, individually and in the churches and ecclesial structures and networks of which we are a part, as entirely the same and equally in need. And yet to make such an admission is the best way to invite God's transfiguring grace into every aspect of our being and doing. The assurance of God's limitless mercy should also encourage us in daring to ask the difficult questions of ourselves which are inevitably raised by our theological understanding of sin. We ask so we might be helped to recognize, and thereby be rescued from, the temptations that inevitably find ways of surfacing: in our formal ecumenical relationships, within our own particular traditions, between leaders and the faithful, and indeed more broadly in our failures as Christians to love one another as Christ loves us, which so undermines our Christian witness to the world

"No testing has overtaken you that is not common to everyone" writes Paul (1 Cor 10:13), and to a considerable degree it seems that the spiritual risks that assail humanity in every time and place can be seen as typified in Christ's own temptations. Turning stone into bread puts the focus on the enticements that arise out of controlling resources and amassing riches; the worship of the kingdoms of the world illustrates the seductive distortions of power and control; and the prospect of leaping from the temple pinnacle only to being caught by angels exemplifies the lure of fame and ego. This is not to say that we must all abjure shouldering positions that bring us into dealings with wealth, authority or status, but to underline the need for continuous caution against what can potentially be good servants becoming bad masters, and thinly disguised idols.

Therefore, we must constantly apply a basic hermeneutic of suspicion to ourselves, asking God to open our eyes to our own susceptibilities to self-deception. As individuals, if we are mature, we will know the value of a good spiritual director, or soul friends who will speak honestly and call us out when appropriate, or of setting in place other robust means of holding ourselves to account within the body of Christ and before the throne of grace. But how good are we at doing this as churches or other Christian institutions? Indeed, it is widely argued that institutions are particularly prone to the risk of prioritizing sustaining their own institutional life over the delivery of their ostensible purposes, and churches are no different.[4]

So what are some of the traps into which we are prone to falling? The bigger, richer, more connected, more powerful or more influential we are (established

---

[4]   See Alasdair MacIntyre, *After Virtue*, 2nd ed. (London: Duckworth, 1985).

churches in particular, beware!), the greater the risks of being compromised in this way, but none are immune. Metropolitan Anthony Bloom once said:

> It seems to me [...] that the Church must never speak from a position of strength. [...] The Church ought to be, if you will, just as powerless as God himself, which does not coerce but which calls and unveils the beauty and the truth of things without imposing them. As soon as the Church begins to exercise power, it loses its most profound characteristic which is divine love: the understanding of those it is called to save and not to smash.[5]

So we must ask ourselves where riches, power and ego can and do distort. Do we seek institutional self-preservation in unhealthy ways – for example, at the deliberate or callously negligent expense of "competitor" church traditions or denominations? Do our structures privilege hierarchy, in practice undermining commitments to servant leadership? How does the dollar bottom line influence our discernment processes and decision making? Do we find it easier to sit and sup with the rich and powerful than to walk with the poor and the marginalized, in our own churches, and in our Christian networking? Do we impose conformity and silence the awkward voices within our ranks that may, or may not, have uncomfortably prophetic words for us?

But we must be open to more insidious distortions too – perhaps telling ourselves narratives of victimhood and the denial of power and status that bring pretences of occupying the moral high ground, and so deliberately rebuffing opportunities for reconciliation with erstwhile oppressors; or declining to step into a more influential role where that is offered. Under- as well as over-privileging of money, status and identity can also distract us from our primary goal of faithful obedience in whatever ways God asks of us.

We can also draw on other spiritual insights in calling out the best in ourselves and one another. Ignatian principles are one example of wisdom from one tradition now being more widely shared, for example in the discernment of spirits.

Being honest together about our need of God's redeeming love at work among us as we desire to cooperate more closely within Europe should help us grow together in new and deeper ways. And yet this also brings less obvious risks that must be named. Sometimes, becoming closer to one partner may inadvertently distance us from another. Or growing closeness with partners in one part of the world may engender imbalances to global relationships, even weakening ties within our church families, which is particularly dangerous in these times of growing xenophobia, nationalism and insularity. These are cautions to bear in

---

[5]   "On the Cross of Our Lord," last modified March 21, 2012, http://www.pravmir.com/on-the-cross-of-our-lord/.

mind, even as we work to overcome the scandal of structural separation within the body of Christ within our own continent.

Walking and talking together, and listening too

"Let us consider how to provoke one another to love and good deeds," we read, "not neglecting to meet together [...] but encouraging one another" (Heb 10:24–25). Grounding our relationships in Christ should remind us he is the eternal Word made flesh, underlining the importance of continuing, honest conversation. We must keep talking, even when we disagree – and then, even more so, we must not merely talk but listen, and do so beyond mere words. This is especially true for individuals and institutions who readily make themselves heard. Big churches must listen to small churches, rich to poor, established to non-conformist, privileged to marginalized, the elite to the uneducated and so on. Hierarchies must bend low enough truly to hear the grass-roots, allowing them to speak uninterrupted from the integrity of their own contexts. More than that, we must create welcoming spaces where those with no voice can express themselves in their own languages (literal and metaphorical), on their own terms. (And here we must not forget the particular voicelessness of our environment, and its susceptibility to ruthless exploitation, with the European ecological footprint particularly damaging.) If we take seriously Paul's assertion that "to each is given the manifestation of the Spirit for the common good" (1 Cor 12:7), we will strive to hold together as widely as possible, as truthfully as possible, as our best defence against our human frailties.

While we can often see the need of this in the discourses of the world, we must also recognize our own requirement to seek out those brothers and sisters in Christ who are given no hearing in our existing structures and practices. The Global Christian Forum challenges ecclesial bodies to ask ourselves: whom, from within the body of Christ are we lacking, as we gather and take counsel together? Whom do we need to receive – and indeed, by whom do we need to be received? Similarly, Receptive Ecumenism tells us we must keep asking: What are we lacking, and what do we need to receive from others? We must make the necessary shift from focusing on what we think we have to share with others (or more starkly, what we think others ought to learn from us!) to asking ourselves what we need to learn from others. Engaging seriously on this basis should enable us to be drawn into more intimate relationship with each other, while at the same time deepening our own authentic identities, in all their distinctiveness.

Though we share much as Europeans, we are often more different than we may at first realize – whether in the various Christian traditions of a particular place, or across our traditions. Our languages and our histories influence our cultures and the mind-sets they shape, and the suppositions we harbour. We have different secularisms, different atheisms, different political theologies. Learning better to listen to one another about all these, and discover new perspectives and insights, also helps us hold up mirrors in which each of us has the opportunity better to understand our own dynamics and motivations. What we thought were neutral assumptions can often turn out to be something else altogether. By determining to hold together, we may find ourselves better able to hear the prophetic voices which discern our blind spots, voices that so often come from those we would rather ignore.

This pursuit of Christian unity and church unity matters, for the sake of the world, in every area of mission and ministry. Jesus Christ calls us to be salt and light (Matt 5:13,14) and prays to the Father for his disciples to "be one, as we are one [...] so that the world may believe" (John 17:11, 21). Our ability truly to stand together colours our common witness, from how effectively we can communicate God's love for God's world in word and practical action, to the capacity of the Christian voice to contribute to public debate at all levels.

Christian unity has come a long way since the 1910 World Missionary Conference, which is often seen as a crucible of the modern ecumenical movement. Called out of the frustrations of European confessional divisions impeding missionary endeavours, it tellingly acknowledged that "divisions within the Christian church weaken its testimony and confuse the total impression made by Christianity on the minds of the non-Christian peoples."[6] They still do so today. The subsequent Life and Work movement, promoting common practical engagement with pressing social questions, and the World Conference on Faith and Order, approaching unity from a more theological perspective, came together in the World Council of Churches. In subsequent decades, multilateral and bilateral ecumenical encounter has broadened and deepened, embracing an ever wider span of contemporary Christianity.

Unsurprisingly, faith and order questions have tended to dominate, since for most of us, it is in matters of doctrine and ecclesiology – or closely related issues – that our separations were grounded, or at least justified for public consumption. But this approach has downsides as well as upsides. It too often directs attention to what divides us, not what unites us, and we must beware of becoming mired in difference and stale in our exchanges. The production of increasingly detailed maps of our divisions does not automatically guarantee a route towards reconciliation.

That said, exploring the dimensions of our differences can enhance mutual understanding and highlight areas of agreement of which we were previously unaware. Such exploration undergirded the formation of United and Uniting

---

[6]   "World Missionary Conference 1910: Section VIII, 7 and 9" quoted in *The Oxford Handbook of Anglican Studies*, ed. Mark Chapman, Sathianathan Clarke, and Martyn Percy (Oxford: Oxford University Press, 2016), 466.

Churches, and remains the bedrock of communion-focused agreements such as Porvoo. Revisiting old questions may alter long-standing and antagonistic perceptions, as with the 1999 Joint Declaration on the Doctrine of Justification by the Lutheran World Federation and the Catholic Church. Looking at today's ecumenical landscape, it is hard to remember that within my lifetime Roman Catholics were forbidden to enter churches of most traditions or even to join in saying the Lord's Prayer.

So the long, painstaking work around doctrine and ecclesiology continues to provide firm foundations upon which can be set vital green lights that unblock old log-jams and set in motion all manner of on-the-ground collaborations. Like the invisible eight ninths of an iceberg below the water-line, it gives substance, ballast, balance and stability to the visible ninth of our common life. It has opened up extensive opportunities for fostering trust, maximizing our liturgical engagement (and praying together changes so much), and liberating our capacity to stand shoulder-to-shoulder on current affairs. Set in the wider context of effective two-way communication including good mutual listening, institutional relationships can be enabled to harness the often considerable energies on the ground of local ecumenical activity. The two should always be mutually encouraging, mutually reinforcing, even if at different times and seasons one or other may appear to be the driving engine.

It is heartening that formal bilateral dialogues have increasingly broadened in recent years to reflect more on common life and action – for example through reflecting on *diakonia*, or on theological anthropology and its implications for contemporary ethical issues. And in many relationships, they are now paralleled by agreements in unity and mission addressing practical ways of drawing more closely together institutionally and in common service of the world. This helpfully subverts earlier risks of professionalizing ecumenism, as the sole preserve of academic theologians and senior clergy. When not "translated" into less technical language and then intentionally conveyed, this work can remain distanced from other Christians, clergy and people alike, who are left with limited awareness of what is under discussion or of the significance of the issues being debated. This is part of the wider challenge of effective communication top-down, and centre-outwards, on all issues, with which churches all too often struggle; and the fuller need for a shared sense of genuine, substantial exchange in both directions.

Common witness and practical action

Whether or not St Francis of Assisi said "Preach the gospel at all times – and if necessary, use words," it is clear that no matter how wonderful our theologizing, it is little more than a clanging cymbal if it does not serve our call to share the good news of Jesus Christ, implicitly and explicitly, in proclamation and in tangible action. "Faith and Order" concerns cannot be separated from "Life and Work", to which we now turn – from the kindnesses of neighbours banding together to help a family in need, to church leaders united in tough political stances.

Anglicans look back to the 1920 Lambeth Conference for the beginnings of a global theology of practical, public and political engagement at both institutional and individual levels. It resolved that:

> The Church cannot in its corporate capacity be an advocate or partisan, 'a judge or a divider', in political or class disputes where moral issues are not at stake; nevertheless in matters of economic and political controversy the Church is bound to give its positive and active corporate witness to the Christian principles of justice, brotherhood, and the equal and infinite value of every human personality.[7]

It affirmed extensive public engagement by Christian individuals alongside that of the institutional church, stating that "Members of the Church are bound to take an active part, by public action and by personal service, in removing those abuses which depress and impoverish human life. In company with other citizens and organizations, they should work for reform [...]."[8] Ecumenical partnership was automatically assumed.

William Temple (Archbishop of Canterbury from 1942 until his death in 1944) enlarged upon this approach in *Christianity and Social Order.* In response to criticism both from within the Church of England and from politicians for taking stands on political and economic questions, he argued that the church was "bound to 'interfere' because it is by vocation the agent of God's purpose, outside the scope of which no human interest or activity can fall." It was therefore the responsibility of the church to "announce Christian principles and point out where the existing social order at any time is in conflict with them. It must then pass on to Christian citizens, acting in their civic capacity, the task of reshaping the existing order in closer conformity to the principles." On this basis, said Temple, "nine-tenths" of the so-called interfering would be done through the influence of individual Christians acting outside the institutional life of the church, for "it is recognized that Christian men and women in the various walks of life should bring the spirit of Christ to bear upon their work."[9] He wrote about Anglicans, and all Christians.

Thus Churches must speak together and act together institutionally, and provide resources – from spiritual anchoring and theological depth, to practical

---

[7]   The Lambeth Conference, "Resolutions Archive from 1920," Resolution 75, accessed February 26, 2019, https://www.anglicancommunion.org/media/127731/1920.pdf.

[8]   The Lambeth Conference, "Resolutions Archive from 1920," Resolution 77, accessed February 26, 2019, https://www.anglicancommunion.org/media/127731/1920.pdf.

[9]   William Temple, *Christianity and Social Order* (London: SCM Press, 1950), 21–22.

structures and direct encouragement – for their members also to speak and act, grasping whatever opportunities come their way. Myriad local initiatives growing out of relationships forged through the Week of Prayer for Christian Unity, or ecumenical Lent Groups, are just one example. On a wider scale is the Conference of European Churches, which grew from a desire to surmount the fragmentation and political divisions of Cold War Europe. Its current work programme focuses on dialogue with European political institutions (including and beyond the EU); peace-building and human rights; citizenship, economic and environmental justice; employment and social issues; bioethics; and issues of migration and asylum; alongside theological and ecclesiological dialogue.

This last matters fundamentally. In practical action and public engagement, we are not merely people of good will with a religious veneer (nor can practical action become a substitute for pursuing the sometimes costly closeness that better preaches Christ the crucified Lord). We are to be bearers of God's redeeming love to a wounded world: it is through Jesus Christ that the world, and ourselves with it, will be changed. Therefore, we need to abide in him, the true vine, in all we do, and in how we do it, every step of the way. Sustaining our spiritual life avoids the risk that common action becomes mere do-gooding. As the Collect from the Church of England's Book of Common Prayer asks, "Prevent [Go before] us, O Lord, in all our doings, with thy most gracious favour, and further us with thy continual help; that in all our works, begun, continued, and ended in thee, we may glorify thy holy Name [...]."[10] This takes us beyond our capacities merely to pursue "Christian principles", so we may not tire in our own strength, and, further, by the Spirit that comes from abiding in Christ, may deliver "fruits that will last", our words and actions echoing into eternity.

Worship and life come together in other ways. The burning fire to pursue social justice is fanned both by Scripture's exhortations and by what might be called the aesthetics of belief. The glorious transcendence into which prayer and worship at times transport us, the numinous presence of God somehow Emmanuel, with us, as we sit and stand and kneel, sing and speak and listen, can conspire to provide a greater vision of divine purpose for a better life for humanity, and the confidence and conviction to pursue it. The more we pray together, the more likely we will know God's empowering Spirit enabling our acting together, from our institutions to our communities.

The churches must continue to encourage those with a particular gift in the hard task of cudgelling the brains that God gives us (and doing so on our knees), so that we may truly learn to "read the signs of the times". We need a deep spiritual wisdom and maturity, in our critique of the world, and in the alternative vision we offer; and to avoid the risks of platitudinous and superficial engagement

---

[10] Crown Copyright, *The Book of Common Prayer* (Oxford: Oxford University Press, 2001, 647.

that buys into the fallen structures of the world. Thus, for example, while we see free will as part of what it means to be made in the image of God, it is not enough to preach about how we exercise choice in the spending of our time, money and attention: we must also critique the system that channels us into the narrow and unhealthy choices of contemporary consumerism. Beyond the injustices within the operation of current economic systems are the injustices, indeed the falsehoods, of the systems themselves, privileging growth over sustainability through assumptions that fail to reflect our planet's finite resources. Similarly, while arguing for sufficient financial resourcing for end of life care, we must reject political rhetoric that reduces the "value" of life to fiscal terms. We must refocus debate on what it means to live as genuinely flourishing individuals, in flourishing societies, harbouring our natural resources sustainably. Developing theological depth together matters, if we are to do all this well. We need the breadth of one another's differing experiences and perspectives; but we also need the grace to listen and speak honestly with one another when we suspect a partner may have read the signs wrongly, and to draw deeply on wells of theological wisdom. It is not always easy to discern where appropriate enculturation slides into inappropriate syncretism. For example, nationally based churches may need the help of external perspectives in order to see where promoting the legitimate flourishing of their people can become distorted by indefensible nationalist tendencies.

Such theological critique also requires effective bilingualism. We speak, listen and learn first among ourselves, from the heart of Christian faith, on Christ's terms; and not merely in theological jargon, but in words that touch the hearts and minds of all our people. But then we must also find words to connect with the wider world. Empowering and encouraging our people to engage with the world, confident their faith is more than adequate to its challenges is what William Temple called for – but which was not sufficiently well done in Wales. Sometimes our role will be to stir up public opinion to press governments to "do the right thing" even where it seems difficult and unpopular. We should be confident in our capacity not only to speak truth to power within our own contexts, but to shape the nature of debate and the dynamics of the public space: changing the very context in which power operates. Rowan Williams' taxonomy of "procedural" and "programmatic" secularism offers compelling resources.[11]

Providing a confident and convincing counter-narrative to the worst sorts of contemporary consumerist secularism's often all too dehumanizing assumptions around human identity is a particularly tough task, from which we dare not flinch – particularly when this provides fuel for populism and racism, for example. We are challenged to find better ways of speaking of the things of God in the language of the world, even the language of the cultures in which our churches are rooted, however wholesome they be. One need is to recognize the power of narrative, over

---

[11]   See Rowan Williams, *Faith in the Public Square* (London: Bloomsbury, 2012), 2–3.

the propositional arguments typical of modernity. Further, narrative returns us to the power of gospel and incarnation, and the living truth that God is Emmanuel, with each of us, whatever our "here and now", thus subverting the gnostic risks of abstract spiritual or religious "principle". It is not just that we learn to tell our own stories: we learn to find our place in the ultimate story of the unfolding of God's salvation through history.

To a considerable degree, Christian leaders share the need of politicians, academics, the broadsheet press and much of traditional public discourse, to hear the neo-Magnificat's call for the mighty to be unseated in the voices of those who say "we've had enough of experts." Churches, especially where informally or formally part of "the establishment", may well be part of the perceived bubble which is disengaged with the lived challenges of those swathes of population who feel marginalized, excluded or deliberately ignored by a dismissive patronizing elite. We must show that Jesus Christ cares and understands the pressures that lead people to feel populist, nationalist answers are the only real hope – including the false soteriologies of Brexit that only this island's plucky little nation state has delivered us from centuries of continental conflicts and two world wars. We must offer practical ways forward that are relevant to their lives, and which tangibly demonstrate we take seriously the difficult circumstances in which racism and populism may gain traction. Austerity, immigration, refugees and asylum seekers, ethnic and national tensions and so forth impinge hard on some individuals and communities. For others, life has been so hard, so hopeless, for so long, that any alternative is worth risking, since things can hardly become worse. Yet we must not just presume to speak for others, however well-meaning we are. As the persuasiveness of the "take back control" slogan indicates, what people need more is genuine agency in their own lives, including in representing their own perspectives on their own terms and knowing themselves heard.

Speaking the language of the world also has risks. My hunch is that post-war efforts to present faith in ways that avoided charges of sentimental or superstitious nonsense too often left no place for the transcendent encounter with the living God, revealed in Jesus Christ, and made present by the Spirit, as heaven touches earth and eternity breaks in on time and space. Forging a new public language for this will be more effective the more deeply it is rooted in the proclamation of transfiguring faith declared in Christian lives. I am confident this is particularly so when Christians who on the surface seem radically different from one another, profoundly demonstrate the Christ-rooted unshakeable foundation of our deeper unity: "see how these Christians love one another."

We best hold fast to each other through holding fast to Christ. This was the experience of the Anglican Church of Southern Africa in the apartheid years. Knowing they stood in firm agreement on the heart of faith enabled them to keep standing together, while holding differing views even on such major issues as how to oppose apartheid, the armed struggle and sanctions. Though life-and-death issues, they were not seen ultimately as church-dividing issues. The world around is desperately in need of good modelling of unity in difference, and if we cannot show it, who will?

Our common life in Christ should therefore honestly name the hard challenges – but also the joys – of wrestling to live with difference and disagreement. Every voice, including hidden and anonymous witnesses, must be sought out and heard. We who own four Gospels must avoid the temptation to seek a single unifying story to explain complex, multifaceted situations, or to close down unfolding dialogue prematurely. Nor may we need simplified, uniform responses. The legitimate diversity of our ecclesial bodies, including both in our theological emphases and our circumstances, may generate an effective spread of complementary responses – a symphony of voices and actions directed by a shared vision. Different experiences, different perspectives, different contexts, must all be respected. And indeed, we do not need to know all the answers. All we are called to be is faithful and obedient. As David Bentley Hart has put it: "One of the temperamental advantages to be gained from a belief in divine providence is serenity in the face of history's ambiguities."[12]

Such distinctiveness notwithstanding, I want to end by touching on the question of what constitutes the goal of our ecumenical endeavours, and admit to alarm when it seems that relationships of "full communion", entailing varying degrees of pulpit and table fellowship and interchangeability of ministries, are becoming an end in themselves. Reconciled diversity between continuing parallel ecclesial jurisdictions with no stated intention to move to closer integration of institutional life, in pursuit of ultimate union, hardly seems to deliver the fullness of Christ's prayer for us to be one. Some may argue this is a realistic assessment of the current lack of enthusiasm within denominations to give up their independent and distinctive existence. But this falls far short of the vision for "full, visible unity" seen by those within the historic ecumenical movement as the ultimate goal; and it seems to me a dereliction of our vocation in Christ "so that the world may believe."

Conclusion

I was a British diplomat for fifteen years prior to ordination, and in the two decades since have striven to find ways of applying skills of cross-cultural communication and reconciliation to bear in the life of Christians and Churches. Yet what fires me most remains the twin focus of the two great commandments: first,

---

[12]   David Bentley Hart, "No Enduring City: The Gospel both Created and Destroyed Christendom," *First Things* 8 (2013), accessed February 26, 2019, https://www.firstthings.com/article/2013/08/no-enduring-city.

growing and helping others grow, in loving God with heart and mind and soul and body; and second, that rubber-hits-the-road complement of living out the calling of faith in the neighbourhood-village of God's world. Answering faith and order questions is not a goal in itself. But I have discovered how vital a long, slow, even painstaking obedience in shared theological and ecclesiological reflections can be, in providing a sure light to our path and lamp to our feet, wherever God calls us to follow. Like invisible roots going deeper and wider than the tree above, it provides strength, support, anchoring and nourishment for all that is visible. It helps us better grasp who we are called to be as children of God, members of the one body of Christ, and of how we should live within creation.

"There is one body and one Spirit, just as you were called to the one hope of your calling, one Lord, one faith, one baptism one God and Father of all, who is above all and through all and in all" (Eph 4:4–6). This is where our unity lies, past, present and future, for the sake of the world. May it be so. Amen.

Bibliography

Anglican Communion News Service. "Archbishop of Canterbury 'Challenge and Hope' for the Anglican Communion." Last modified June 27, 2006. https://www.anglicannews.org/news/2006/06/archbishop-of-canterbury-challenge-and-hope-for-the-anglican-communion.aspx.

Chapman, David, and Sathianathan Clarke, and Martyn Percy, eds. *The Oxford Handbook of Anglican Studies.* Oxford: Oxford University Press, 2016.

Crown Copyright. *The Book of Common Prayer.* Oxford: Oxford University Press: 2001.

GCF. "Global Christian Forum." Accessed February 26, 2019. http://www.globalchristianforum.org/.

Hart, David Bentley. "No Enduring City: The Gospel both Created and Destroyed Christendom." *First Things* 8 (2013). Accessed February 26, 2019. https://www.firstthings.com/article/2013/08/no-enduring-city.

Lambeth Conference. "Resolutions Archive from 1920." Accessed February 26, 2019. https://www.anglicancommunion.org/media/127731/1920.pdf.

MacIntyre, Alasdair. *After Virtue.* London: Duckworth, 1985.

Pravmir. "On the Cross of Our Lord." Last modified March 21, 2012. http://www.pravmir.com/on-the-cross-of-our-lord/.

Temple, William. *Christianity and Social Order.* London: SCM Press, 1950.

Williams, Rowan. *Faith in the Public Square.* London: Bloomsbury, 2012.

8. The Church of England and European Ecumenism: Making our Unity Visible

Will Adam, Matthias Grebe and Jeremy Worthen

The Church of England's relations with churches in Continental Europe might be described as a pattern composed of various threads, interweaving and connecting with one another in numerous ways. While each thread would have certain parallels in the case of other European churches, the pattern that emerges from them is distinctive, reflecting the particular geographical, social and ecclesial position of the Church of England as this has been shaped through its history. What could be termed the density of the pattern arises at least in part from the deliberate cultivation by the Church of England of a European presence and of European relationships. That engagement acquired a new focus in the twentieth century, following two world wars whose origins were in the European Continent, and in which the United Kingdom fought both against and alongside other European countries.

The first section of this paper seeks briefly to sketch out the distinctive pattern made by these interweaving threads of relationship. The second section then explores why the Church of England has sought over the past century to develop that pattern in specific ways as a major component of its participation in the ecumenical movement. The third and fourth sections examine in more detail some of the challenges in the contemporary context for the way that pattern has developed. The fifth and final section looks to outline a fresh approach to European ecumenism that draws on the strengths of existing relationships and the structures that support them.

Current pattern of relations

An initial distinction might be made between four different threads that connect the Church of England to churches in Continental Europe: the Diocese in Europe, local links, the Conference of European Churches, and formal church-to-church agreements. In this first section of the paper, a brief overview is offered of each of these, though it is important to note at the outset that the treatment of them will not be equal. The last requires more extended explanation than the first three. In all of them, however, the principle of breaking down barriers by means of personal contact, encounter and dialogue between members of different churches is fundamental.

Diocese in Europe

For centuries, the Church of England has had a presence in Continental Europe, the focus being on providing chaplaincies for English people living abroad. In 1842, chaplaincies in southern Europe were brought together within the new Diocese of Gibraltar, although chaplaincies in northern and central Europe continued to be under the jurisdiction of the Diocese of London. They finally came together in 1980 to form the present Diocese of Gibraltar in Europe, generally referred to as the Diocese in Europe.[1] This means that the Church of England is itself a church that crosses the English Channel and the North Sea (as they are called from the English side), with bishops who serve communities across Continental Europe as members of its College of Bishops and full representation of the Diocese in its General Synod. There would be parallels as well as contrasts with the various ways in which other European churches support networks of "diaspora" congregations across Europe, not least in England itself. While a substantial proportion of the Diocese in Europe's chaplaincies are in the European Union (EU), its presence in Morocco, Turkey, Russia, Norway, Switzerland, Iceland and the Balkan states is a reminder that Europe also extends far beyond it.

As well as ensuring that Europe has a significant place within the Church of England's structures and general consciousness, the Diocese in Europe provides numerous opportunities for building relationships of practical cooperation in mission and ministry between its chaplaincies and neighbouring churches on the Continent. These will vary, not least because of the differing ecclesial relationships between the Church of England and those churches. Where the Church of England is in communion with those churches, then such cooperation can include ordained ministers from another church being licensed by the bishop to serve in the Church of England. In other contexts, the focus may be on working together to address social challenges, as has happened in Athens where the Anglican

---

[1]   See "Diocese in Europe," accessed February 13, 2019, https://europe.anglican.org/. On the long history of positive relations between the Church of England and Lutheran and Reformed churches in Northern Europe, see for instance Norman Sykes, *Old Priest and New Presbyter: The Anglican Attitude to Episcopacy, Presbyterianism and Papacy since the Reformation* (Cambridge: Cambridge University Press, 1956), chapter 6, "The Times of Ignorance".

chaplaincy has been in partnership with the Orthodox Church to provide support for those affected by economic hardship and for refugees.[2]

The continental chaplaincies of the Church of England are not the sole expression of Anglicanism in continental Europe. The Episcopal Church (TEC) also maintains chaplaincies under the title the Convocation of Episcopal Churches in Europe, overseen by a bishop of TEC based in Paris. There are also, in the Iberian Peninsular, two extra-provincial dioceses under the metropolitical authority of the Archbishop of Canterbury, namely the Lusitanian Catholic Apostolic Evangelical Church (in Portugal) and the Spanish Reformed Episcopal Church. Both these churches grew from small groups of Catholic clergy and lay people who broke away from the Catholic Church in the nineteenth century. They were both overseen from the Church of Ireland for a number of years before becoming extra-provincial dioceses in 1980.

Local links

The second thread in this pattern of relationships is more informal. Over the course of the last hundred years, numerous local links have been established between Church of England dioceses and their counterparts on the Continent, between cathedrals in England and on the Continent, and between parishes, sometimes under the umbrella of diocesan links, and sometimes through town-twinning arrangements. It is hard to provide accurate data in this area because of the more informal character of these relationships, which may lie dormant for a while before being re-ignited by new enthusiasm. They include relationships with Roman Catholic churches as well as with Protestants.[3]

Such links serve a crucial purpose in enabling members of the Church of England based in England to experience at first hand an encounter of fellowship with other Christians that crosses both ecclesial and national borders. For many, this has been very powerful and something they have come to value highly. At diocesan level, there may be a more conscious focus on mutual learning alongside sharing in fellowship and prayer. There may also be a strong civic dimension, as there is for instance in the way that the relationship between Coventry Cathedral and the Frauenkirche in Dresden is situated within the partnership between the two cities established in the wake of the bombing of both during the Second World

---

[2]   See Jean Mertzanakis, "Working Together – a Report by Jean Mertzanakis," accessed February 13, 2019, http://anglicanchurchathens.gr/working-together-a-report-by-jean-mertzanakis/.

[3]   See the Anglican – Roman Catholic Committees of France and England, *Twinning and Exchanges: Guidelines Proposed by the Anglican – Roman Catholic Committees of France and England* (London: CIO, 1990).

War.[4] There are other local links that date from the post-war years where the desire for the churches to contribute to peace and reconciliation across a Continent shattered by conflict was a significant factor.

Conference of European Churches

The third thread in this pattern is also bound up with conflict, though from a different era. The Conference of European Churches (CEC) came into existence in 1959.[5] At a time when the chilling effects of the Cold War were being felt across Europe, it brought together churches from both sides of the Iron Curtain, which meant a meeting of Protestant and Orthodox as well as a meeting of East and West.[6] The Church of England was a founding member of CEC, which includes three "groupings" of churches: Orthodox, Protestant, and Anglican and Old Catholic, within which the Church of England is a significant presence. Anglicans have an especially critical role in the context of CEC because of the way they combine an appreciation of the inheritance of the Protestant Reformation with a commitment to "Catholic order" from the first millennium of the church's history, including the historic episcopate. Members of the Church of England have held key positions within CEC, with Bishop Christopher Hill and Dean John Arnold among its former Presidents.

In the context of Brexit, it is important to note that CEC includes member churches from both within and outside the EU, and that it engages with the Council of Europe as well as with the EU institutions. It thereby provides an opportunity to issue statements and speak into the institutions of both the EU and wider representative bodies. Moreover, the UK will, for now at least, remain a member of the Council of Europe and play a part in the European Court of Human Rights. The Human Rights discourse, based in the Council, is of great significance and one into which churches in the UK could seek to play a stronger part.

Formal agreements

The fourth thread in the pattern of the Church of England's relations with Continental churches is the formal agreements it has made. While there are many

---

[4]   See Frauenkirche Dresden, "The Coventry Cross of Nails," accessed February 13, 2019, https://www.frauenkirche-dresden.de/en/cross-of-nails/.

[5]   See "Conference of European Churches," accessed February 13, 2019, http://www.ce ceurope.org/.

[6]   Lucian N. Leustean, *The Ecumenical Movement and the Making of the European Community* (Oxford: Oxford University Press, 2014), 57–90.

parallels between these agreements, they also differ from one another. It will therefore be helpful to present them separately first, before offering some comments on the pattern created by all four threads considered together.

The most long-standing of these relationships is with the Old Catholic Churches of the Union of Utrecht, dating from the Bonn Agreement of 1931.[7] This not only predates the establishing of the next such formal relationship by 60 years but is also rather different from the other examples. It predates both the Second World War and the post-war European project and, moreover, extends to the whole of the Anglican Communion, of which the Church of England is a member.[8]

By comparison with later texts, the Bonn Agreement itself is very brief, and yet it also establishes what for Anglicans is the weightiest of ecclesial relationships: that of churches in communion with one another. It also thereby created something of an anomaly on both sides because of the geographical overlap between episcopal jurisdictions. If two churches both hold to the ideal of one bishop for the one church in each place, and are fully in communion with one another, why should they continue to support two bishops for two different sets of Christian communities in the same place? Finally, it might be noted that the Old Catholic Churches are mainly but not exclusively based within the EU, with a large Old Catholic presence in Switzerland.

The Meissen Common Statement, including the Declaration signed in 1991, sets out the formal relationship between the Evangelical Church in Germany (EKD) and the Church of England, committing each other to journeying towards greater unity and closer fellowship.[9] The Common Statement is a result of ecumenical dialogue between those who lived through World War II. Indeed, it was written in direct response to the events of Coventry and Dresden, already referred to, by those who learned from this experience, and it was signed soon after German reunification, which paved the way for the re-incorporation into the EKD of the *Landeskirchen* located in the former East Germany. From the very beginning, the idea of establishing a formal relationship between the Church of

---

[7] See Union of Utrecht of the Old Catholic Churches, "Relations with the Anglican Church," accessed February 13, 2019, https://www.utrechter-union.org/page/294/relations_with_the_anglican_chur.

[8] There is a collection of statements from the international Anglican – Old Catholic dialogue on the Anglican Communion website, accessed February 25, 2019, https://www.anglicancommunion.org/relationships/churches-in-communion.aspx. These include "Belonging Together in Europe: A Joint Statement on Aspects of Ecclesiology and Mission," issued by the Anglican – Old Catholic Co-ordinating Council in 2011.

[9] The English text of Meissen Conversations, "On the Way to Visible Unity: A Common Statement," 1988, is available on the Church of England's website at https://www.churchofengland.org/sites/default/files/2017-11/meissen_english.pdf.

England and the EKD was considered in the context of the need for strengthening reconciliation within Europe and building a new kind of European society.

The Meissen relationship is therefore one that has practical and social purposes at its very heart. The Common Statement focuses on the church as sign, instrument and foretaste of the Kingdom of God. Highlighting the importance of *koinonia*, it sets out the churches' commitment to strive for "the full visible unity of the body of Christ on earth", and is designed to bring together not only bishops, but also priests, pastors, and parishes from both nations. Unlike the Bonn Agreement, however, it does not establish a relationship of ecclesial communion between the Church of England and the EKD. The critical issue here is the commitment of the Anglican Communion to sharing in the historic episcopate as integral to its understanding and practice of such relationships. The *Landeskirchen* within the EKD have a variety of structures for oversight and expression of personal *episcope*, and there are evident differences in history and understanding regarding the episcopate. Most visibly, the absence of a full ecclesial communion prevents the inter-changeability of ordained ministers between the two churches. The Common Statement, however, frames the relationship thus established between the churches as an important step on the journey towards full visible unity, which will include such communion: it is not the destination, and the Common Statement commits the churches to a continual striving for the goal.

The Porvoo Communion came into being five years later in 1996, with the Porvoo Common Statement providing the basis for an agreement of communion signed between the Anglican Churches of the British Isles and the Nordic and Baltic Lutheran Churches.[10] The Lutheran churches of Denmark and Latvia were not among the original signatories, through subsequently the Church of Denmark, the Lutheran Church in Great Britain and the Latvian Evangelical Lutheran Church Abroad have joined the Porvoo Communion. As with Meissen, at the beginning the relationship encompassed churches that until very recently had been on opposite sides of the Iron Curtain; the Cold War cast a lingering shadow here too. For the present, most of the Lutheran member churches lie within the EU, though Norway and Iceland sit outside it.

As with the Old Catholic Churches of the Union of Utrecht and by contrast with the EKD, the Porvoo Agreement established relationships of ecclesial communion for the Church of England. This is expressed by the participation of Anglican bishops in the consecrations of Lutheran bishops, and the participation of

---

[10] For the text of the Porvoo Common Statement together with valuable supplementary material, see Conversations between the British and Irish Anglican Churches and the Nordic and Baltic Lutheran Churches, *Together in Mission and Ministry: The Porvoo Common Statement with Essays on Church and Ministry in Northern Europe* (London: Church House Publishing, 1993). More recent documents relating to the Porvoo Communion may be found at the website for the Porvoo Communion, http://www.porvoocommunion.org/.

Lutheran bishops in the consecration of Anglican bishops. It also means that at local level clergy can assist in one another's churches, including presiding at the eucharist. The possibility also exists of Anglicans being appointed to posts in Lutheran churches and vice versa.

Five years after the signing of the Porvoo Agreement and ten years after Meissen, in 2001 the Declaration attached to the Reuilly Common Statement was signed. This is a formal agreement between the French Protestant Churches (Lutheran and Reformed) and the Anglican Churches of Britain and Ireland, committing themselves to witness and service together.[11] Inspired by the positive reception of the Meissen and Porvoo Agreements, it is framed like Meissen as a stage along the way to ecclesial communion, which will enable interchangeability of ordained ministers. Work continues on what mutual "recognition" and "reconciliation" of ministries might mean both for Anglicans and for those in the Reformed and Lutheran traditions.

Much is also, however, already possible in terms of cooperation at local level. Currently, under the Reuilly Agreement, five pilot sites in France have opted to deepen the relationship between Diocese in Europe chaplaincies and French Protestant churches: Nice, Lyon, Paris, Grenoble and Lille. This has found practical expression in initiatives such as offers to share buildings, weekly prayer meetings that take place between various church leaders, and the hosting together of an Alpha Course. It might be noted that in the French context, both Anglicans and Protestants are minority churches, whereas under the Meissen and Porvoo agreements the Church of England is often relating to others that have also historically been "majority" churches of various kinds and may continue to be so.

Gaps in the pattern?

As had already emerged during this brief survey, the four threads just reviewed connect with one another in a number of different ways. Formal agreements open up new opportunities for local cooperation with neighbouring churches on the part of Diocese in Europe chaplaincies. Local links may also be situated in the wider context of those agreements, as Church of England dioceses for instance forge relationships with *Landeskirchen* within the EKD, through participation in synods, delegation visits, the German Kirchentag, prayer letters, and through diocesan, deanery and parish exchanges, which may include ministers, church workers and students. The presence of Diocese in Europe chaplaincies in countries

---

[11]   See Conversations between the British and Irish Anglican Churches and the French Lutheran and Reformed Churches, *Called to Common Witness and Service: The Reuilly Common Statement with Essays on Church, Eucharist and Ministry* (London: Church House Publishing, 1999).

where Orthodoxy is strong creates bonds of respect and understanding that contribute to CEC's ability to bring together its very wide range of member churches in witness to Christ.

Two weaknesses might be noted in this pattern, in terms of how well it connects the Church of England with the life of Continental Christianity. The first is the absence of formal relationships with Roman Catholicism on the Continent. While local links and the work of the Diocese in Europe provide numerous opportunities to strengthen personal and communal ties, CEC was formed before the entry of Roman Catholicism into the mainstream of the ecumenical movement at Vatican II, and there are significant factors in the maintenance by the Catholic Bishops' conferences of their own, separate European structures, COMECE (the Commission of the Bishops' Conferences of the EU) and CCEE (the Council of European Bishops' Conferences).[12] Moreover, the kind of formal agreements that the Church of England has established with European churches stemming from the magisterial stream of the sixteenth-century Reformation are simply not possible in the case of the Roman Catholic Church. The third and fourth threads, therefore, cannot contribute to strengthening relations by the way they interweave with the first two.

The second weakness concerns what might broadly be termed Evangelical and Pentecostal churches that do not form part of historic Protestant denominations in Continental Europe. One of the features of English ecumenism in recent decades has been a determined attempt to include such churches within ecumenical structures and initiatives so far as possible, with considerable – though not unqualified – success. While the successful expansion in membership of Churches Together in England has been critical to this, the Church of England has been very much committed to that cause. While numerical strength of Evangelical and Pentecostal churches across different European countries will vary significantly, many are growing and may continue to do so. Yet they are unlikely to be picked up by any of the four threads just listed, except for initiatives in local cooperation from the Diocese in Europe. If relationships here with the Church of England are to grow across the European Continent, it is likely to require a re-imagining of one or more of the other threads, or indeed a new kind of thread altogether.

The significance of Europe for Anglican ecumenism

As already noted, the existence of the Diocese in Europe commits the Church of England, as it participates in the ecumenical movement, to building relationships

---

12 See "The Catholic Church in the European Union," accessed February 13, 2019, http://www.comece.eu/site/en/home, and "Consilium Conferentiarum Episcoporum Europae," accessed February 13, 2019, https://www.ccee.eu/.

with its neighbours on the Continent. Other factors, however, are clearly also involved. The cultivation of local links and the establishing of formal agreements, with the support for the church relationships that flows from them, demand time, energy and resources from the participants. Why has the Church of England devoted so much of these things to relationships that have little impact on the great majority of its own members, who live in England?

To answer that question, it might be best to begin by rehearsing the reasons for paying attention to relationships with other churches at all. The classic approach of the ecumenical movement has been to focus on the concept of unity, as the first of the credal marks of the church.[13] Ecumenical endeavour explores and illuminates the depth of this dimension of the church that is God's gift, facing the challenges of the disunity that is always growing like tares amidst the wheat within "God's field" (1 Cor 3:9), the church, because of human sin and failure. Through such endeavour, it seeks the renewal of the whole church and its fruitfulness in mission.

Ecumenical activity over the last hundred years may be characterized by two interrelated foci: first, making visible the unity of the church, by addressing its present divisions and separations; and second, animating the church's witness to the unity of humanity, by acting together against enmity, injustice and indifference to the suffering of others. The relation between these two might be articulated with reference to the statement from the Second Vatican Council that "the Church is in Christ like a sacrament or as a sign and instrument both of a very closely knit union with God and of the unity of the whole human race."[14] The unity

---

[13]   See e.g. Yves Congar, *Diversity and Communion*, trans. John Bowden (London: SCM, 1984); Carl E. Braaten and Robert W. Jenson, eds., *In One Body through the Cross: The Princeton Proposal for Christian Unity. A Call to the Churches from an Ecumenical Study Group* (Grand Rapids, Michigan: Eerdmans, 2003); Paul Avis, *Reshaping Ecumenical Theology: The Church Made Whole?* (London: T&T Clark, 2010).

[14]   Vatican II, *Lumen Gentium*, Dogmatic Constitution on the Church, 1964, no. 1, http://www.vatican.va/archive/hist_councils/ii_vatican_council/documents/vat-ii_const_19641121_lumen-gentium_en.html. One might also note the profound connection between the unity of the human race and the unity of the church expounded by Henri de Lubac on the basis of patristic sources in *Catholicism: Christ and the Common Destiny of Man*, trans. Lancelot C. Sheppard (London: Burns and Oates, 1950). On church as sacrament more generally, see e.g. Anglican – Roman Catholic International Commission: "The Church as *koinonia* requires visible expression because it is intended to be the 'sacrament' of God's saving work. A sacrament is both sign and instrument," Introduction to the *Final Report*, 1981, § 7, available at http://www.anglicancommunion.org/media/105260/final_report_arcic_1.pdf. More recently, there is a careful discussion of this important theme in World Council of Churches' Commission on Faith and Order, *The Church: Towards a Common Vision*, Faith and Order Paper 214 (Geneva: World Council of Churches, Commission on Faith and Order, 2013), §§ 25–27.

of God's redeemed people is both sign and instrument of unity between the nations from which they come, as constituted by persons created together in the image and likeness of God and redeemed together by the blood of Christ.

These two foci correspond with the "Faith and Order" and "Life and Work" streams within the ecumenical movement of the last hundred years. Both are vital for ecumenism: although to some extent they can proceed independently from one another, they cannot ultimately be detached from one another either.[15] The "sacramental" quality of the church's unity corresponds to the truth that the church is called by God from and for the sake of the whole world. Ecumenism that is content to look at inter-church relations as a self-contained zone of activity is undermining an adequate ecclesiology, which must be in dialogue with missiology. Equally, an ecumenical activism of justice and peace that is based on assertions of human solidarity and grows impatient with the demanding, long-term work of overcoming ecclesial division cannot sustain ecclesial action in the world – the action of churches together in communion with one another – but risks ending up with nothing but the efforts of individual activists, however well-placed and influential they may be. The real dynamism of ecumenism derives precisely from its ability to connect these two foci together: making visible the unity of the church and animating the church's witness to the unity of humanity, with each gaining power from the other.

That dynamism is evident in some features of the pattern of relationships between the Church of England and churches in Continental Europe surveyed in the preceding section. Initiatives have arisen in response to the desire to witness to the unity of humanity after two world wars, by truthful remembrance, practices of reconciliation and commitment to the ways of peace. Church relations also sought to maintain the affirmation of common humanity in the context of a Cold War that dehumanized in more subtle ways the people on one side in the eyes of those on the other. As an action of the church, however, that witness has included the visible expression of the church's unity in the face of enmity, callousness and injustice: through shared worship and prayer, through discipleship and learning the way of Christ together, and through enabling the gathering of Christians from different nations and churches around a single eucharistic table and even the sharing of ordained ministers from one church in the life of another. The Meissen relationship is perhaps particularly strong example of how the two basic foci of the ecumenical movement have been brought together in a dynamic way, but others could be given too.

---

[15] Anglican – Reformed International Commission, *God's Reign and Our Unity. The Report of the Anglican – Reformed International Commission 1981–1984* (London: SPCK, 1984), §§ 15–24.

Witnessing to the unity of humanity

One of the reasons that European ecumenism has been able to be effective in this way over the course of the last century is the deep connection that has remained in many cases between church and nation. The two world wars and - though somewhat differently - the Cold War that followed them pitted nations against nations within Europe. The challenge of the churches in witnessing to the unity of humanity was therefore crucially about upholding human and ecclesial solidarity across national boundaries, which coincided in many cases to a significant extent with confessional boundaries between the majority churches of different nations. Churches that retained some kind of claim to "represent" their nations - such as the Church of England - were in a unique position to bring together the two foci of ecumenical activity by building relationships across national boundaries that also served to some extent as confessional boundaries, thereby both making visible the unity of the church and witnessing powerfully to the unity of humanity. Such an approach was apparent in much of the ferment of ecumenical activity that took place between the two world wars.[16] European ecumenical relations, therefore, have always had as one horizon throughout the last hundred years that of seeking to enable European nations to live peaceably together, in a way that affirms both national diversity and human unity.

The continuing influence of the "Christendom" ideal of one church for one nation might also be perceived in the more recent history of European ecumenism. It seems unlikely to be accidental, for instance, that apart from the French Protestant churches of the Reuilly Agreement, the Church of England's formal agreements have tended to be with churches where this ideal is also to some extent part of the historical legacy: not only the Nordic Lutheran churches and (rather less straightforwardly) the EKD, but also the Old Catholic Churches of the Union of Utrecht, among whom the goal of a properly "national" Catholic Church had played a significant role until it was overwhelmed by the traumas of the Second World War. Moreover, the characterization of the Diocese in Europe's congregations as chaplaincies offering ministry to English speakers reflects an implicit assumption that within Continental Europe - uniquely in the global Anglican Communion - responsibility for mission that reaches out to the whole community belongs to the historic church of the nation in that place, and that it would not be right for Anglicans to seek to share in that responsibility by planting "indigenous" churches either independently or in partnership with others. The ideal of one

---

[16] See for instance J. H. Oldham, ed., *The Churches Survey Their Task: The Report of the Conference at Oxford, July 1937, on Church, Community, and State* (London: George Allen & Unwin, 1937), and, on the ecumenical vision of Nathan Söderblom in particular, Kjell Blückert, *The Church as Nation: A Study in Ecclesiology and Nationhood*, European University Studies (Frankfurt am Main: Peter Lang, 2000).

church for one nation, supplemented, if necessary, by special arrangements for "diaspora" groups, still haunts a significant part of the European Christian imagination. This may help to explain the weakness of specifically European relations for the Church of England with Roman Catholicism on the one hand and "free church" Evangelicalism and Pentecostalism on the other. For very different reasons, this historic ideal simply does not hold the same resonance for them, and indeed may have negative associations with oppressive and discriminatory behaviour in the past and the present.

The Christendom ideal may also account for another feature of European ecumenism. It was stated above that the hope animating the ecumenical movement has been for the renewal of the whole church and its fruitfulness in mission, through its growth in unity. Yet missional activity and prayer for renewal have not in the past had a high profile in the Church of England's extensive engagements in European ecumenism. The model of relationships between distinct national churches may account for low expectations regarding what has been regarded elsewhere as the fruit that ought to follow from significant growth in ecumenical relations: the horizons for mission and renewal have been set within national church borders, not across them within Europe as a whole. It might be noted at this point that mission and renewal could be constructive points of departure for ecumenical conversation across Europe with both Roman Catholicism and "free church" Evangelicalism and Pentecostalism.

It is not only the continuing unravelling of European Christendom that suggests that the way in which European ecumenism has been effective in the past cannot be expected to keep bringing similar benefits in the future. The end of the First World War is now over a hundred years ago, and the devastation of the Second World War is receding from living memory. Peaceful relationships between the European nations appear well-established, with no immediate threat of conflict. Instead, tension within nations is more likely to attract attention, with deep divisions spilling over into populist politics in countries that might have been considered just a short time ago as models of political stability, as discussed elsewhere in this volume. Such divisions are bound up in all kinds of ways with transnational and international relations. Global developments, economically and politically, have effects on the life of nations that they can appear powerless to resist, as with the "financial crash" of 2008 or the "migration crisis" of 2015. While transnational and international institutions might present themselves as necessary ways to manage such global forces, they may nonetheless be perceived as undermining both the sovereign authority of nation states and the kind of cohesion and belonging that nation states need in order to thrive.

This still evolving social and political situation is significantly different from the context that generated the ecumenical endeavours outlined in the first part of this paper, which is not to say that they have nothing left to offer or that nothing can be learnt from them. The question about the theological understanding of nations and states to which ecumenists gave careful attention between the wars, for instance, may need to come back into focus again.[17] The differences here are, however, a strong indicator that simply continuing the trajectory set for European ecumenical relations in the twentieth century may leave European ecumenism in a neglected by-way as the twenty-first century unfolds. Witnessing to the unity of humanity today requires the churches to advocate justice and compassion effectively across national boundaries in the response of European societies to migration, most obviously, but also to economic globalization. It requires patient listening with regard to the concerns that many people feel in those societies about community, identity and belonging in the face of changes perceived as coming from beyond their borders and beyond their control, changes that may indeed be far-reaching in their effects. In this context, building relationships between churches across national divides that also correspond to some extent with confessional divides does not in and of itself carry the same symbolic power or practical effect as it did when the primary challenge was conflict between nation states still emerging from Christendom in Europe.

Making visible the unity of the church

If the challenges of witnessing to the unity of humanity in Europe now look quite different from the periods in which European ecumenism secured its most notable achievements, there is a further set of issues regarding the work of making visible the unity of the church, associated with the Faith and Order strand within ecumenism. Influenced by Anglican ecumenism, much of the emphasis here has been on progressing towards full visible unity by certain formal stages.[18] Yet progress on this front appears to have stalled, at least in Europe. It is difficult to envisage how it can proceed much further in the foreseeable future with Roman Catholicism or with Orthodoxy, while the Church of England so far has shown itself incapable of imagining how it could move into ecclesial communion with churches that do not already have some form of commitment to and practice of the historic episcopate, i. e. almost all European Protestant churches except for those Lutheran churches already within the Porvoo Communion. Discussion of

---

[17] Nigel Biggar, *Between Kin and Cosmopolis: An Ethic of the Nation* (Cambridge: James Clarke, 2014).

[18] For a concise summary of this approach, see Gregory K. Cameron, "Four Principles of Anglican Engagement in Ecumenism," section 3, "The Processes of Ecumenism." The text may be found in *The Vision Before Us: The Kyoto Report of the Inter-Anglican Standing Commission on Ecumenical Relations 2000–2008*, ed. Sarah Rowland Jones, 2009, 31–34, accessed February 25, 2019, https://www.anglicancommunion.org/media/107101/the_vision_before_us.pdf.

current proposals for communion with the Methodist Church in Britain are high-lighting again the obstacles that this route has repeatedly faced over the past hun-dred years.[19] Meanwhile, new churches are proliferating across Europe, many of them broadly Pentecostal in character, many with roots outside Europe in Africa or the Americas, and most with an ecclesiology that does not easily fit with the guiding assumptions of the Faith and Order movement within ecumenism, including that of proceeding via a series of stages towards full visible unity.

One of the reasons for this is that newer churches in Europe are unlikely to share what could be called the dominant narrative of European ecumenism: a nar-rative about how unity has been lost, what unity regained would be like, and the stages through which we need to pass in order to get there. It is arguable that every social movement needs some such narrative about past failures, the future ideal and the steps that can be taken here and now that will lead us towards it. It has always been a critical difficulty for the ecumenical movement, however, that the story about how Christian unity was lost in Western Europe in the sixteenth century is told very differently by Protestants and Catholics.[20] The 500th anniver-sary of the Protestant Reformation in 2017 was an important opportunity to re-flect on that, as well as listening to voices within European Christianity for whom the story they want to tell is rather different: the Orthodox, for whom what hap-pened in sixteenth-century Western Europe is only one episode in a much longer history of Christian division, and "revivalist" churches who are seeking to recreate directly the church of the New Testament and may not see any of this history as their story at all.[21]

Parallel differences could be traced regarding the other elements of the dom-inant narrative of European ecumenism on the visible unity of the church. There would be quite different accounts of what the goal looks like and about the best way to advance towards it, even within the denominations that have shaped the ecumenical movement of the past hundred years.[22] Anglican thinking on ecumen-ism helped to shape a fragile consensus in Faith and Order ecumenism in the final decades of the twentieth century, that the journey could proceed through progres-sive mutual recognition by churches of baptism (so we stand together as followers

---

[19]   See Faith and Order Bodies of the Church of England and the Methodist Church, *Mission and Ministry in Covenant*, available at https://www.churchofengland.org/sites/default/files/2017-10/mission-and-ministry-in-covenant.pdf.

[20]   Jeremy Worthen, "The 500th Anniversary of the Reformation: An Ecumenical Event?" *Theology* 120/2 (March / April 2017): 100–107.

[21]   For an Orthodox perspective, see Andrew Louth, "Orthodox Reflections on the Reforma-tion and its Legacy," *One in Christ* 15.2 (2017): 314–333.

[22]   Natan Mladin, Rachel Fidler, and Ben Ryan, *That They May All Be One: Insights into Church-es Together in England and Contemporary Ecumenism* (London: Theos, 2017), 20–22; report also available at https://www.theosthinktank.co.uk/cmsfiles/Reportfiles/CTE-report.pdf.

of Christ), eucharist (so that we can share together in the sacraments) and ministry (so that we receive one another's ordained ministers).[23] It is not so much that the consensus has been disrupted by alternative accounts, as that members and leaders of Christian churches within and beyond those that led the ecumenical movement in Europe are no longer inclined to invest time, energy and resources in work on this project.

Towards an ecumenism of common action

Is it possible to imagine a fresh approach within Europe to the first focus for ecumenism, making visible the unity of the church, that does not hinge on such a narrative? One might attempt to start in a different place, for instance, by affirming that what makes the church's unity visible in the world is participation in common action that expresses our common life in Christ. The foundation for all our attempts to grow in our relations with one another is the conviction that the life we have in Christ as the gift of the Holy Spirit is a common life, in which we are members one of another. It is this theological reality that lies at the root of ecumenical endeavour. It is not that we share – or do not share – a common historical narrative, or cultural assumptions, or set of priorities for action, but that we have a common life, and as those who have died with Christ and live in union with him, we have no other. This common life is lived in common action that includes public prayer and celebration of the sacraments, evangelization and the making of disciples, and the work of witnessing to the unity of humanity against division, conflict, marginalization and injustice. Given that all these things belong to our common life in Christ, that which truly makes visible our unity in him must encompass them all and relate them to one another. We witness to the unity of humanity in our shared sacraments and in our common prayer and praise. We proclaim the Good News of reconciliation in our joint action for justice and peace. While the phrase "ecumenism of action" is not a new one, the current formulation hinges on common action that expresses the common life of the church, which means that the agency of the church needs to be clear.[24] It concerns what churches

---

[23]   World Council of Church's Commission on Faith and Order, *Baptism, Eucharist and Ministry*, accessed February 25, 2019 https://www.oikoumene.org/en/resources/docu ments/commissions/faith-and-order/i-unity-the-church-and-its-mission/baptism-eucha rist-and-ministry-faith-and-order-paper-no-111-the-lima-text.

[24]   Archbishop Justin Welby, "Ecumenical Spring," speech at World Council of Churches 70th Anniversary, 16 February 2018, at https://www.archbishopofcanterbury.org/ speaking-and-writing/speeches/ecumenical-spring-archbishop-justins-speech-world-council-churches.

do in their plurality such that they act as one body, one church, and thereby potentially re-configure and transform that plurality.

If the unity of the church becomes visible through participation in common action that expresses the church's common life, then the primary questions for ecumenism are not determined by narratives about the losing or gaining of unity. Instead, they hinge on discernment in the present moment. Three interrelated dimensions of that discernment might be identified: participants, action, and means of participation. First, then, who are the ecclesial participants in this conversation about enabling our unity to be made visible in common action? Who is already part of it, and who may there be in this place who also shares in our common life in Christ, yet is not contributing to it? And if some are not included, is that because there are good grounds for restricting the conversation to a small number of partners, or is it because in our heart of hearts we actually still believe that like-mindedness and similar cultural attitudes are the best basis for common action, and not communion in the Triune God? Was there a free choice by some to turn down an invitation to join, or have those inside set up barriers to discourage outsiders, directly or indirectly? Whose gifts are we missing, and whose voice is lacking?

Second, what might be the common action in this place that would express more fully our common life in the Spirit, the gift of Jesus Christ? It may be that action uniting different churches is already happening, in which case the priority may be to nurture and sustain it, not keep trying to start new things. Still, is what we are doing together sufficient to express the truth that we are members of one another (Rom 12:5)? To what extent does the common action we currently share include prayer, praise and the celebration of the sacraments? To what extent does it include the proclamation of the gospel and supporting disciples in learning the way of Christ? To what extent does it give space for common witness to the peace and reconciliation that flow from the cross into every part of human life? How can we act together as churches in such a way that we do these things as the church, as one church, with one faith, one baptism, and one Lord, in the power of the one Spirit? One might also ask about who is able to participate in such common action. Clearly it is likely to involve those who represent their churches in a publicly recognized way, but it is vital that there are opportunities for church communities to engage directly.

Third, what means of participation do we need so that all who share in the life of Christ in this place can act together and speak together in the name of Christ? Such means may include meetings of small numbers of people who through dialogue and conversation build relations of trust, respect and honesty that can radiate outwards to change the way that different Christian communities perceive one another. They may extend to formal agreements about practical cooperation, covering the sharing of buildings or the investing of resources in joint projects. They may require councils, assemblies or committees, study groups or theological commissions. They may involve statements that express mutual recognition of baptism, eucharist and ministry; the historic priorities of the Faith and Order movement continue to have an important place. Churches exist in the contingencies of human history as institutions of various kinds, some small and some great, some ancient and some very new, and it is therefore necessary that what makes their unity visible will have institutional aspects to it. The kind of ecumenical structures and relationships we need, however, are those that facilitate and flow from common action that expresses common life in Christ. That means they must be congruent with the dynamics of common life in the body of Christ. Moreover, unity is not made visible simply by the existence of these structures and relationships, but only by the action that they support. What matters is not primarily progress in generating and extending the structures enabling participation, but action that gathers all participants in the common life of Christ in one place together to share in the work of Christ.

What it means to be "in one place" is one of the long-term challenges for European ecumenism. The "places" of human communities and societies are, to some extent at least, the imaginative constructions of human culture, whose power to shape deep assumptions about identity and belonging changes over time and varies between members of the same community, as has been explored elsewhere in this volume. Can we, however, speak of Europe as "one place" for the church? Where does it end, and is it conceivable that the churches of Europe as a whole could engage in meaningfully *common* action at all? Yet the unity of Europe as human place is also signified by the coming together of different human places within it, different communities and societies, in ways that reflect and celebrate a sense of connectedness rooted in intertwined geography and history. To return to the analysis in the first part of the paper, CEC is in a unique position alongside COMECE and CCEE to enable the common action of the churches in Europe: its existence affirms that Europe is indeed a single "human" place, with all the diversity it encompasses, and therefore also a space for the churches to act together as the church. The Church of England's Diocese in Europe connects Christian communities in towns and cities across the Continent with one another and holds them together with the Church of England, thereby in a more limited if also very focused way sustaining a sense of Europe as a common place for the church of Christ. Local links and formal agreements, by joining this community to that community, this church to that church, across national borders in Europe, speak in a different register of Europe as a place within which common action may express the common life of the church, making visible its unity to the world.

The rich texture of European ecumenical relationships of which the Church of England is a part all constitute valuable "means of participation" in common action that expresses our common life. Yet perhaps the critical development needed at the present moment is to seek ways of building on what has already been established to open up conversations that include a wider range of ecclesial voices, and in particular the voices of those who may not easily locate themselves in the story of European ecumenism that focuses on the development of institutions and the signing of historic agreements, or in the wider "faith and order" narrative of progressive mutual recognition around baptism, eucharist and ministry. The European churches need the participation of those who do not necessarily see themselves as "European" in the same sense as those churches who claim a continuity in place here stretching back over centuries, but instead e. g. as European participants in a worldwide fellowship whose origin and centre may lie in another of the world's Continents. Without their active presence, it is not possible to make visible the unity of the church in Europe in a way that speaks of the unity of humanity at this juncture in its history. The churches need to show in their unity a human unity that does not depend on the acceptance of a dominant cultural narrative, but rather on the recognition of the creator's image in every human person and on the capacity of human persons to come together across cultural barriers, including those of language, in celebration and protest, in work and rest.

The three dimensions of the discernment being advocated here as the characteristic practice of an ecumenism of common action are inseparable from one another. Welcoming new participants to the conversation goes hand in hand with being ready to extend the scope of the common action that expresses the common life we rejoice to share. It cannot be assumed that it will have little to do with worship or discipleship. An ecumenism of common action should sustain the hopes and prayers of the ecumenical movement for the effectiveness of the church in mission and for its renewal through the sharing of gifts. The goal of the ecumenical movement is the visible unity of the church, that is, the unity of the church in action in the world. Such action requires the support of structures and commitments, institutions and agreements, if it is to be sustained over time. It cannot be assumed, however, that the institutions and agreements we have now are the only ones we need for the future, or that they provide the template for whatever comes next, or that their simple existence represents the achievement of visible unity. New forms of common action, with new circles of participating churches, may require new means of enabling participation; new wineskins for new wine.

Bibliography

Anglican – Old Catholic Co-ordinating Council. "Belonging Together in Europe: A Joint Statement on Aspects of Ecclesiology and Mission." https://www.anglicancommu nion.org/relationships/churches-in-communion.aspx.

Anglican – Roman Catholic Committees of France and England. Twinning and Exchanges: Guidelines proposed by the Anglican-Roman Catholic Committees of France and England. London: CIO, 1990.

Anglican – Reformed International Commission. God's Reign and Our Unity. The Report of the Anglican – Reformed International Commission 1981–1984. London: SPCK, 1984.

Anglican – Roman Catholic International Commission. Final Report, 1981. http://www.anglicancommunion.org/media/105260/final_report_arcic_1.pdf.

Avis, Paul. *Reshaping Ecumenical Theology: The Church Made Whole?* London: T&T Clark, 2010.

Biggar, Nigel. *Between Kin and Cosmopolis: An Ethic of the Nation.* Cambridge: James Clarke, 2014.

Blückert, Kjell. *The Church as Nation: A Study in Ecclesiology and Nationhood.* European University Studies. Frankfurt am Main: Peter Lang, 2000.

Braaten, Carl E., and Robert W. Jenson, eds. *In One Body through the Cross: The Princeton Proposal for Christian Unity. A Call to the Churches from an Ecumenical Study Group.* Grand Rapids, Michigan: Eerdmans, 2003.

Commission of the Bishops' Conferences of the EU. "The Catholic Church in the European Union." Accessed February 13, 2019. http://www.comece.eu/site/en/home.

"Conference of European Churches." Accessed February 13, 2019. http://www.ceceurope.org/.

Congar, Yves. *Diversity and Communion.* Translated by John Bowden. London: SCM, 1984.

Conversations between the British and Irish Anglican Churches and the French Lutheran and Reformed Churches. Called to Common Witness and Service: The Reuilly Common Statement with Essays on Church, Eucharist and Ministry. London: Church House Publishing, 1999.

Conversations between the British and Irish Anglican Churches and the Nordic and Baltic Lutheran Churches. Together in Mission and Ministry: The Porvoo Common Statement with Essays on Church and Ministry in Northern Europe. London: Church House Publishing, 1993.

Council of European Bishops' Conferences. "Consilium Conferentiarum Episcoporum Europae." Accessed February 13, 2019. https://www.ccee.eu/.

"Diocese in Europe." Accessed February 13 2019. https://europe.anglican.org/.

Faith and Order Bodies of the Church of England and the Methodist Church. Mission and Ministry in Covenant. https://www.churchofengland.org/sites/default/files/2017-10/mission-and-ministry-in-covenant.pdf.

Frauenkirche Dresden. "The Coventry Cross of Nails." Accessed February 13, 2019. https://www.frauenkirche-dresden.de/en/cross-of-nails.

Leustean, Lucian N. *The Ecumenical Movement and the Making of the European Community.* Oxford: Oxford University Press, 2014.

Louth, Andrew. "Orthodox Reflections on the Reformation and its Legacy." *One in Christ* 15.2 (2017): 314–333.

Lubac, Henri de. *Catholicism: Christ and the Common Destiny of Man.* Translated Lancelot C. Sheppard. London: Burns and Oates, 1950.

Meissen Conversations. "On the Way to Visible Unity: A Common Statement," 1988. https://www.churchofengland.org/sites/default/files/2017-11/meissen_english.pdf.

Mertzanakis, Jean. "Working Together – a Report by Jean Mertzanakis." Accessed February 13, 2019. http://anglicanchurchathens.gr/working-together-a-report-by-jean-mertzanakis/.

Mladin, Natan, Rachel Fidler, and Ben Ryan. *That They May All Be One: Insights into Churches Together in England and Contemporary Ecumenism.* London: Theos, 2017.

Oldham, J. H., ed. *The Churches Survey Their Task: The Report of the Conference at Oxford, July 1937, on Church, Community, and State.* London: George Allen & Unwin, 1937.

"Porvoo Communion." Accessed February 13, 2019. http://www.porvoocommunion.org/.

Rowland Jones, Sarah, ed. *The Vision Before Us: The Kyoto Report of the Inter-Anglican Standing Commission on Ecumenical Relations 2000–2008*, 2009. https://www.anglicancommunion.org/media/107101/the_vision_before_us.pdf.

Sykes, Norman. *Old Priest and New Presbyter: The Anglican Attitude to Episcopacy, Presbyterianism and Papacy since the Reformation.* Cambridge: Cambridge University Press, 1956.

Union of Utrecht of the Old Catholic Churches. "Relations with the Anglican Church." Accessed February 13, 2019. https://www.utrechter-union.org/page/294/relations_with_the_anglican_chur.

Vatican II. Lumen Gentium, Dogmatic Constitution on the Church, 1964. http://www.vatican.va/archive/hist_councils/ii_vatican_council/documents/vat-ii_const_19641121_lumen-gentium_en.html.

Welby, Justin. 'Ecumenical Spring', speech at World Council of Churches 70th Anniversary, 16 February 2018. https://www.archbishopofcanterbury.org/speaking-and-writing/speeches/ecumenical-spring-archbishop-justins-speech-world-council-churches.

World Council of Church's Commission on Faith and Order. *Baptism, Eucharist and Ministry.* https://www.oikoumene.org/en/resources/documents/commissions/faith-and-order/i-unity-the-church-and-its-mission/baptism-eucharist-and-ministry-faith-and-order-paper-no-111-the-lima-text.

World Council of Churches' Commission on Faith and Order. *The Church: Towards a Common Vision, Faith and Order Paper 214.* Geneva: World Council of Churches, Commission on Faith and Order, 2013.

Worthen, Jeremy. "The 500th Anniversary of the Reformation: An Ecumenical Event?" Theology 120/2 (March / April 2017): 100–107.

9. "Let us be Peacemakers": Christian Presence and Witness in Europe[1]

Justin Welby

The papers collected together in this volume had their genesis in a conference held at Lambeth Palace under the title "After Brexit: European Unity and the Unity of the European Churches". The occasion for this conference was an official visit to London by the Chair of the EKD Council, Landesbischof Heinrich Bedford-Strohm and the President of the EKD Synod, Dr Irmgard Schwaetzer. The timing of the visit was significant in two ways: first, because it fell between the United Kingdom's Remembrance Sunday on 11 November and the German equivalent, Volkstrauertag, falling a week later. 2018, of course, made these dates doubly significant as the United Kingdom and Germany looked back to the Armistice and the end of the First World War. But the timing was also significant for reasons that the organizers could not have predicted. In the increasingly acrimonious debate on the details of the United Kingdom's withdrawal from the EU, two government ministers, including the Secretary of State at the Department for Exiting the European Union, resigned from the government on the day before the conference and more Conservative MPs delivered letters of no-confidence in the Prime Minister as leader of the Conservative Party.

In this paper, an earlier version of which I gave as an address at the Assembly of the Conference of European Churches on 3 June 2018, I set out a vision for the churches of Europe as brokers and champions of peace and as messengers not of fear, but of Resurrection hope. Fear is the greatest danger that afflicts Christian witness and presence. It is fear of the Other that causes us to put up barriers, whether within churches, between churches and for that matter between nations. It is fear of the Other the causes us to build walls, whether spiritual or physical. It is fear of the Other that leads to divisions and eventually to the fall of civilizations.

---

[1] A previous version of this paper was given at the Assembly of the Conference of European Churches, Novi Sad, Serbia, 3 June 2018. Available online at www.archbishopofcanter bury.org/news/latest-news/let-us-be-peacemakers-europe-archbishop-tells-church-lead ers-serbia.

Christianity in Europe

A Christian presence has existed in Europe since halfway through the first century AD. It has survived the persecutions from the Roman Empire, it has continued through what are often in England called the Dark Ages: the early medieval period in which different tribes from outside the Empire successively overran the Western Empire after the deposition of the last Emperor in 476. It has even survived its own internal dissensions, including the wars in Europe of the sixteenth and seventeenth century which killed more than one third of the population of Germany. It survived the destruction of Europe in the 1940s. It survived in Eastern Europe under persecution between the Second World War and 1989 and I remember smuggling bibles with my wife into Romania and what was then Czechoslovakia during this "Cold War" period. Christians in Serbia have suffered greatly, and the links with the Church of England, older even than the 180 years of diplomatic relations, bear witness to the compassion between Christians at times of war and persecution. There have been recent difficulties and periods of war that cause destruction and pain, especially for those whose task is to proclaim the Gospel of the Prince of Peace. Christianity in Europe does not depend on the organization or governance of the Church, nor does it depend on the virtue of Christians, or the blessing of circumstances; it is assured because it depends on God who raised Jesus Christ from the dead.

In AD 410 the City of Rome was invaded and sacked by Goths. In the years that followed, and in reaction to this moment, St Augustine of Hippo started to write the book that was to dominate his literary output for the remainder of his life. *City of God* or, in Latin, *De civitate dei contra paganos*, is set against the background of pagan despair at the fall of Rome. The gods of that age in whom the people trusted proved not to be able to protect the city from its overthrow. Europe is not today in danger of falling. And there is no sense in which I suggest that Brexit (however this might be lived out) or other crises currently around will derail the European Union or bring about the downfall of Europe. To suggest that would be akin to the old English saying that when there is fog in the Channel then the continent is cut off. However, Europe, like other parts of the world, is in a fragile phase and current geo-political uncertainty is unsettling. In my part of the continent there is a nation attempting to leave the EU; on the other edges of the EU such as the Western Balkans there are countries and peoples keen to get in. For Augustine the fall of Rome showed the specious nature of putting faith in the earthly city. For Augustine the benefit of being a Christian is citizenship of an eternal city. This comes through faith in Christ.

That said, the fact that Christianity survived in Europe does not indicate that it is indestructible, but that God protects the Church that he created and loves. Christian survival within Europe is not an objective of the Church, rather it should be for the Church to be obedient to the pattern of Christ, to be Christ's hand, mouth and love in this world today. Jesus told his disciples that they were to be salt and light,[2] that is: both the means of preserving the society in which the Church exists and also the source of illumination that reveals both shadow and truth, that unveils what seeks to be hidden, and illuminates what inspires.

For the Church to be effective and to continue to be blessed by God, it must speak truth to the societies that it sees around it and act in a way that is consistent with the truth it speaks. One of my own priorities as Archbishop is the renewal of prayer and the monastic life. In Serbian Orthodoxy, for instance, we see the prayer of the liturgy calling all to the face of Christ and we see renewed growth in the life of the monasteries, a true foundation of any society that seeks to be healthy.

Luther referred to the Church as both justified and sinful (***simul justus et peccator***). Taking that into account, how should the Church act and witness in the Europe of the twenty-first century, where the threats are war and terrorism, indifference, individualism and (potentially) economic crisis?

Community

The first thing is community. In the early sixth century, following the fall of the Western Empire, Saint Benedict, one of the patron saints of Europe, founded the first of his monasteries at Monte Cassino. The Rule of Saint Benedict, one of the most inspired and brilliant codes of conduct for any religious community (and, indeed, for any community), provided a flexible and imaginative way of life that attracted tens of thousands of people into its obedience over the next centuries. The Benedictine monasteries sought to be places where the virtues were practiced in humility, with hospitality, and in service to one another, imitating Christ. Above all, they aimed to be places where the lives of the members of the community were lived (and ended) as journeys toward Christ. Not by design but as a collateral and unintended benefit, the Benedictine monasteries and the other religious orders that sprang up preserved European civilization and learning; recreated diplomacy; started universities, schools and hospitals; and provided the foundations of the learning that broke through in the Renaissance.

History would indicate, and the command of Jesus direct, that the Church is first to seek to be a holy community, based in order, in mutual love, in humility, service and hospitality. That all sounds good and harmless, but it is in fact something that runs directly contrary to much of what we see going on in Europe today. Populist calls to preserve our way of life against the other, to put up walls and barriers, to smother dissent and disagreement, to ignore international obligations recognized as morally binding since Jesus spoke of the Good Samaritan: all these will be deeply challenged and will be hostile to a church that is truly itself

---

[2]   Matthew 5:13–16.

hospitable. On the very small stage of Lambeth Palace in London, where we welcomed a Syrian Muslim family of refugees, driven from their homes under shellfire, wounded and harried, the hate mail we received demonstrated the unpopularity even of small gestures.

Presence and witness

Secondly the Church's presence and witness must be more powerful in its unity than the centrifugal forces within Europe are powerful in their fractures. Our ecumenical endeavours are not for the sake of organizational tidiness but so that the Church is a faithful presence and witness.

The Church breaks across boundaries and frontiers as if they did not exist. By being in Christ, I am made one by God in a family that stretches around the world and crosses cultural, linguistic and ecumenical frontiers, driven by the Spirit who breaks down all the walls that we seek to erect. My second priority as Archbishop is reconciliation. We are Ambassadors of Christ and, as such, we should be the sweet scent of holy love and reconciliation. The gift of reconciliation must call the church to unity, and thus we value greatly the CEC, and the work of ecumenism.

Reconciliation is also far more than that: it draws us into seeking to be peacemakers, for they will be blessed and called the children of God.[3] Reconciliation is immensely costly, for it involves paying for sin, and was only created by the death of Christ on the cross. It is a journey of generations, for our historic resentments and hatreds rise in rebellion within our hearts. It is not agreement on all things, for that is impossible, but the acceptance of diversity and even disagreement but yet love in all things. Let us be the peacemakers of Europe, for in making peace we will demonstrate the presence of Christ to those who do not see Him, and we will be the present taste of Christ in a world of individualism, conflict, manipulation and hatreds.

It is no longer the case that to be English is to be Anglican, to be French is to be Catholic, to be Swedish is to be Lutheran, to be Romanian is to be Orthodox. There are Catholics and Protestants, Orthodox and Anglican, Pentecostal and Evangelical Christians in all our countries. For that matter, there are also Muslims, Hindus, Buddhists, and many of no faith at all. That diversity is one of the gifts of the Europe of the European Union, but living with that diversity, especially when diversity becomes division, shows us both the need for reconciliation and the call to the church to be agents and ministers of reconciliation. The more that people are gripped by fear of the Other, and the more that those fears are played on and manipulated by political leaders, the more the Church is called to witness and presence in society, demonstrating the hospitality, the humility, the service and

---

[3]   Matthew 5. 9.

the love in a disciplined and virtuous life which was so clearly demonstrated in the Benedictine monasteries, and which after a thousand years brought back to life the hope of a flourishing humanity.

Some would argue that the EU has been the greatest dream realized for human beings since the fall of the Western Roman Empire. It has brought peace, prosperity, compassion for the poor and weak, purpose for the aspirational and hope for all its people. But it has always been challenged and always will, and others would say that the EU has lost its original vision, its sense of human dignity and its respect for history. They point to the cruelty of the treatment of indebted countries after the recession, to the absence of a moral code or reference to European Christian heritage in the draft constitution. They say that it has become a vehicle for materialism, not a gift to peace building. To some extent both are right and both are wrong. It is clear that the EU needs fundamental reform and a spirit-lifting, history-embedded, people-respecting new vision. Churches must play their part. Brexit is only one of a number of challenges that Europe is facing and may well not be the most serious. It is complicated, but, that notwithstanding, a church that is confident in Christ, that hears the call of the Holy Spirit of God to presence and engagement across Europe, and that lives in the virtues of service, humility and hospitality, will be a church whose presence is assured and whose witness challenges human beings to higher standards of behaviour and calls them to faith in Christ: faith that is the route to salvation.

In its search for unity the Church challenges the divisions of our societies, in its hospitality it challenges selfishness and fear of the other, in humility it can show how to acknowledge failure but to forgive and seek forgiveness. As Benedict saw, and Augustine dreamed, in such virtues human flourishing is founded.

List of Authors

The Revd Dr Will Adam is the Archbishop of Canterbury's Ecumenical Adviser and also works in the Council for Christian Unity of the Church of England. He was ordained in 1994 and served as a parish priest, most recently in London, before joining the senior staff at Lambeth Palace in early 2017. Throughout his ministry he has been involved in promoting reconciliation and unity between churches. Will retains a parish ministry as an honorary assistant priest in a rural parish in West Sussex and is Editor of the Ecclesiastical Law Journal.

Professor Grace Davie is professor emeritus in the Sociology of Religion at the University of Exeter UK. She is a past-president of the American Association for the Sociology of Religion (2003) and of the Research Committee 22 (Sociology of Religion) of the International Sociological Association (2002–06). In 2000–01 she was the Kerstin-Hesselgren Professor at Uppsala, where she returned for extended visits in 2006–7, 2010 and 2012, receiving an honorary degree in 2008. She has also held visiting appointments at the École Pratique des Hautes Études (1996) and at the École des Hautes Études en Sciences Sociales (1998 and 2003), both in Paris. Her latest publications include *Religion in Britain: A Persistent Paradox* (Wiley-Blackwell 2015) and *Religion in Public Life: Levelling the Ground* (Theos 2017). In addition she was a co-ordinating lead author for the chapter on religion in *Rethinking Society for the 21st Century, Volume 3: Transformations in Values, Norms, Cultures* (CUP 2018), which is the report of the International Panel on Social Progress (see https://www.ipsp.org/).

The Revd Dr Matthias Grebe is a priest in the Church of England and the Advisor for European Church Relations at the Council for Christian Unity. He is currently associate priest at St Edward, King and Martyr in Cambridge and holds a research fellowship at the University of Bonn, working on a project on theodicy. Past publications include *Election, Atonement, and the Holy Spirit* (2014).

Professor Piers Ludlow is professor of international history at the London School of Economics. A historian of post-war Europe, he has written extensively about the historical development of the European integration process and of Britain's problematic relationship with it. His last book was about Roy Jenkins and the European Commission Presidency; his next will be an attempt to provide an overview and an interpretation of Britain's 40+ years as an EC/EU member state.

The Very Revd Dr Sarah Rowland Jones has been Dean of St Davids since May 2018. After reading Maths at Cambridge University, she joined the diplomatic service, and in the following 15 years had postings in the British Embassies in Jordan and Hungary. Responsibilities during London postings at the Foreign Office included energy policy, counter-terrorism and dealing with the European Union. She left the service in 1996 for training, then ordination, within the Church in Wales. She has since lived in South Africa, working as Research Adviser to successive Archbishops of Cape Town, and during this time completed a doctorate in philosophy of religion and public theology, entitled Doing God in Public. She serves on various regional and international Anglican and ecumenical bodies.

Ben Ryan is Head of Research at Theos. He is the editor of *Fortress Britain? Ethical Approaches to Immigration Policy for a Post-Brexit Britain* (JKP 2018) and the author of a number of Theos reports including *A Soul for the Union* (Theos, 2015) on the development of the European project form Christian democratic origins to its current state. He holds degrees in European politics from the London School of Economics and in Theology and Religious Studies from Cambridge. Outside of Theos he is a trustee of Caritas Social Action Network.

Prof Dr Arnulf von Scheliha is Professor for Theological Ethics at the University of Münster and Director of the Institute for Ethics and Associated Social Sciences, a post he has held since 2014. He studied theology, philosophy and history in Kiel, Munich and Tübingen and read for his doctorate at the University of Kiel. He was ordained in the former North Elbian Evangelical Lutheran Church and has held posts at the Universities of Hamburg, Osnabrück and Basel (Switzerland) as well as at the University of the German Armed Forces in Hamburg. His principal research interests are in political ethics and religious policy; ethics of peace; ethics of medicine; ethics of environment; interreligious hermeneutics; history of modern theology.

The Most Revd and Rt Hon Justin Welby became the Archbishop of Canterbury in 2013. He was previously Bishop of Durham, Dean of Liverpool Cathedral and a Canon of Coventry Cathedral, where he worked extensively in the field of reconciliation. Before he began training for ministry in 1989, Archbishop Justin worked